WHAT OTHERS ARE SAYING ABOUT THIS BOOK:

"I read and reread everything you sent me. Thanks for writing such a revealing book (*Why Christians Get Sick*). It is one every preacher should read."
    – Pastor David M. Helmic, Potts Camp, Mississippi

"Dear Rev. Malkmus: Your Book *Why Christians Get Sick* is terriffic!
    – Dr. Nathan M. Meyer, President, Bible Prophecy Association, Ohio

"Our patients are really benefiting from your book *(Why Christians Get Sick).*"
    – Dr. Michael Lebowitz, Cedaredge, Colorado

"We commend you for your courage in addressing this controversial subject. Many Christians, no doubt, will reject the message of this book, preferring to remain in their idolatrous relationship to food and tradition . . . We, like everyone else, must face this issue, and take responsibility for our own health. This book will help all of us to do that! . . . Thank you for not only addressing the issue, but for living the example."
    – Jack & Carol Barber, owners Waterwise, Inc., Leesburg, Florida

"I have just finished reading the book on *Why Christians Get Sick.* I agree that this is the greatest next to the Bible. It opened my eyes to many things. I had been searching for a book like this for a long time."
    – Rev. E.S.Bell, Coraopolis, Pennsylvania

"I have just finished reading your book *Why Christians Get Sick.* You certainly hit the nail right on the head, and in such a clear and readable way . . . For the last 22 years my husband and I have devoted our lives to helping others know the natural laws of health, and ways of healing not using the drug and surgical methods we once treated our patients with . . ."
    – Dr. Agatha M. Thrash, M.D., Seale, Alabama

"I cannot tell you what a blessing your book has been for me! After being ill for most of my life, plagued with allergies, asthma, no-name illnesses and with the modern-day medical world trying to treat symptoms instead of finding the causes, I gave up on them and I too looked for answers on my own . . . I have always believed in taking care of the body and eating healthy, but when I discussed it with fellow Christians they just dismissed it . . . With your book (*Why Christians Get Sick*) and its Biblical references I feel secure and have been able to get my (and the Lord's) point across . . . So well in fact that I am to do a class on Christians & Nutrition for our Women's Group . . . I think you have a wonderful ministry! Keep up the excellent work!"
    – Robin Thomsen, Cedaredge, Colorado

"Thank you for writing *Why Christians Get Sick.* My studies in this area led me to similar conclusions."
    – Pastor Paul R. Knierim, Belpre, Ohio

"I recently read your book *Why Christians Get Sick* and I wanted to let you know how much I enjoyed it. I will be recommending it to many of my clients to read."
    – Vickie J. Karnos, Nutritional Consultant, Ridgecrest, California

"Your book *Why Christians Get Sick* has been a true blessing to me."
    – Pastor Glen L. Suydam, Pikwitonei, Manitoba, Canada

"I was thoroughly delighted by your book, *Why Christians Get Sick*... I am a nutritionist and have long had the dream of helping my fellow Christians with nutrition advice. You and I are in agreement on the ideal diet. You have weeded out the bad and kept the good. I commend you on your excellent work!"
    – Dr. Jana D. Bogs, Kamuela, Hawaii

"Your book *(Why Christians Get Sick)* is absolutely fascinating! I could hardly put it down. Thank you so much for sharing your experiences! Also, I very much enjoy your newsletters. These letters along with your programs and seminars provide excellent educational opportunities for anyone interested in good health . . . I share with you an enthusiasm for healthy eating and a desire to help spread the 'good news' about health."
    – Julie Seward, Elizabethton,Tennessee

AND WHAT OTHERS ARE SAYING ABOUT
THE DIET RECOMMENDED BY REV. MALKMUS:

"HALLELUJAH! Praise the Lord! It really worked for me! I am so glad I attended your important seminar last month. The seminar convinced me to change my ways of eating. I agree with you on strict diet, because it is the only way for our IMMUNE SYSTEM to improve to the 100-percent level. For more than 30 years I have had duodenal ulcers. Upon my doctor's advice, I had been taking 500 mg of Tagonet every night before bedtime and whenever necessary. One hundred tablets of 500 mg Tagonet cost about $75 to $80. Not only that, I was also taking 4 to 6 Rolaids almost every day. Well Praise the Lord, after following the HALLELUJAH ACRES DIET for only a short time, I no longer need to take any medication. And not only that, the arthritis in my right elbow is almost gone completely. What's more – I am sleeping better than ever, and no longer have to take laxatives. And all of this has happened in less than one month. . . Before changing my diet, I didn't even realize how much I could enjoy eating salads and fruit – I love them so much! May the Lord Bless Your Ministry . . . HALLELUJAH AGAIN!"
    – Joseph Cohen, Woodbridge, Virginia

"After four weeks on the Hallelujah Diet, all infection (from diabetes) was gone and my prostate problem was all gone. My soreness in the urinary tract was gone for the first time in two years ... Going on this diet has been the greatest thing that has ever happened to me."
    – Rev. Gale Galloway, pastor of Central Baptist Church in Lindale, Texas. In addition to diabetes and serious prostate problems, Rev. Galloway has recovered from severe osteo-arthritis (which required two hip transplants), two heart attacks, toxic poisoning from medication prescribed by doctors, a blood clot that destroyed a quarter of his left lung and a four-day coma from which he was not expected to awaken. After eight months on the Hallelujah Diet, Rev. Galloway said he has not had re-occurances from any of these medical problems, and he has lost more than 85 pounds. (Rev. Galloway's testimony is included in Issue #11 of *Back to the Garden*. See the back of this book for how to receive a free subscription to this newsletter, published by Hallelujah Acres.)

WHY CHRISTIANS GET SICK

by
REV. GEORGE H. MALKMUS

HALLELUJAH ACRES PUBLISHING
EIDSON, TENNESSEE 37731

The nutritional and health information in this book is based on the teachings of God's Holy Word—the Bible, as well as personal experiences and research by the author. The author and publisher do not offer medical advice or prescribe the use of diet as a form of treatment for sickness without the approval of a health professional.

Because there is always some risk involved when changing diet and lifestyles, the author and publisher are not responsible for any adverse effects or consequences that might result. Please do not apply the teachings of this book if you are not willing to assume the risk.

If you do use the information contained in this book without the approval of a health professional, you are prescribing for yourself, which is your constitutional right, but the author and publisher assume no responsibility.

Library of Congress Cataloging in Publication Data
Malkmus, George H.
   Why Christians Get Sick
   1. Christian 2. Health 3. Food, Raw - Therapeutic use.
Library of Congress Catalog Card No. 88-081200
ISBN 0-929619-01-3 Softcover

First Printing 1989	Sixth Printing 1994
Second Printing 1991	Seventh Printing 1994
Third Printing 1992	Eighth Printing 1994
Fourth Printing 1993	Ninth Printing 1995
Fifth Printing 1993	

Printed in the United States of America
All Bible quotations are taken from the authorized **King James Version.**

Published and Distributed by
HALLELUJAH ACRES PUBLISHING
EIDSON, TENNESSEE 37731

"THAT THY WAY MAY BE KNOWN UPON EARTH, THY SAVING HEALTH AMONG ALL NATIONS." (Psalm 67:2)

"FOR I WILL RESTORE HEALTH UNTO THEE, AND I WILL HEAL THEE OF THY WOUNDS, SAITH THE LORD..." (Jeremiah 30:17)

"BLESS THE LORD, O MY SOUL: AND ALL THAT IS WITHIN ME, BLESS HIS HOLY NAME. BLESS THE LORD, O MY SOUL, AND FORGET NOT ALL HIS BENEFITS: WHO FORGIVETH ALL THINE INIQUITIES; WHO HEALETH ALL THY DISEASES; WHO REDEEMETH THY LIFE FROM DESTRUCTION; WHO CROWNETH THEE WITH LOVING-KINDNESS AND TENDER MERCIES; WHO SATISFIETH THY MOUTH WITH GOOD THINGS; SO THAT THY YOUTH IS RENEWED LIKE THE EAGLE'S." (Psalm 103:1-5)

DEDICATED TO

The Loving Memory of

Susanna Marie Hamilton (My Birthday Girl)

Born — February 12, 1973
Died — December 15, 1987
Age 14

ACKNOWLEDGEMENTS

I wish to acknowledge the wonderful help of those who offered suggestions, provided materials, made oodles of corrections, did proofreading, and constantly encouraged me. Without their help and encouragement, this book would not have been possible!

Michelle Austin
Jack and Carol Barber
Carolyn Cocks
Robert and Judith Carballo
Rev. Paul Dow
Rev. and Mrs. Glen Hamilton
Bill and Helen Luce
Janet Malkmus
Marge Porterfield
Rev. David E. Strong

My sincere appreciation to Frank Cunningham and all the beautiful people at East Tennessee Printing for their invaluable help in getting this book printed. Also, Wayne Allen for the cover design.

EAST TENNESSEE PRINTING CO.
210 Washington Street
Rogersville, Tennessee 37857

TABLE OF CONTENTS

INTRODUCTION

Each year, approximately 25,000 people die on the highways of America because of alcohol! Because of the personal loss of loved ones, Mothers Against Drunk Drivers (MADD) was established to enlighten the American people to the dangers of drinking and driving.

Certainly alcohol is a scourge on the American people and I applaud all who try to expose this carnage and reduce alcohol related deaths and injuries.

However, there is another scourge in America. Only this one is taking the lives of millions of Americans each year and over half of them are Christians! Yet there seems to be no voice or organized effort crying out against this unnecessary loss of millions of lives, many who are dying in the very prime of life!

Each year, over 1,000,000 (one million) Americans die from heart disease while over a half-million die from cancer! Most of these deaths are absolutely unnecessary! But why are there not voices crying out against this needless waste of lives and exposing this carnage?

The obvious answer to that question is that most people do not realize that sickness and disease are not necessary and can be avoided! Yes, heart disease, cancer, stroke, diabetes and a host of other diseases can be eliminated if Christians will return to the Bible and observe the natural laws God gave man thousands of years ago!

This book delves into the question of **Why Christians Get Sick** and then goes on to give the biblical answer! Yes, this book tells how Christians can avoid sickness and disease while experiencing superior health!

As Mothers Against Drunk Drivers united to expose the unnecessary loss of life through alcohol, so must Christians arise and unite to expose the unnecessary loss of millions of lives to heart disease, cancer, stroke, diabetes, etc. each year! With the knowledge in this book, we can stop this waste of human lives! May God raise up multitudes of Christian warriors to expose this scourge!

This book will help you to understand the problem as well as the solution! May God bless you.....open your eyes.....illuminate your mind.....and help you to understand as you read! Then, with knowledge, love and the power of God, may we go forth united to help others understand **Why Christians Get Sick** and show them how they too can avoid sickness and disease and experience superior health!

FOREWORD

Can you spare a few hours of your valuable time? You can read this book in just a few hours, **and those few hours could change your life!!!**

There are many good books on "health" available today. But not one of them tells us what **God's Word** has to say about it! My friend and fellow-preacher of the gospel, Rev. George H. Malkmus, has done this in his book. He, as you will read, is **living proof** that practicing God's principles of health does remove sickness and provide energy and desire to serve God faithfully, all the days of our lives.

This book is God's answer to the pantheistic "Holistic Health" that is increasingly being absorbed into the "New Age Movement." Please consider the Scriptures presented and prayerfully make them a part of your life. Be a "Noble Berean" and "See if these things be so!"

I became interested in the scriptural principles of this book as a pastor visiting and listening to the woes of the sick, with health gone, money gone, eating more pills than food, and scared and bewildered. I contrasted their bitter end with that of the Old Testament Fathers who "Gathered up (their) feet into the bed, and yielded up the ghost, and (were) gathered unto (their) people." (Genesis 49:33) They had all their mental faculties, were apparently without sickness or pain, and peacefully, joyfully, went home to be with the Lord. **Some contrast!!!**

Is it possible to escape the pain, astronomical medical bills, and loss of our faculties experienced by the majority of us and, instead, be energetic, productive and happy until God takes us home? Yes! Yes!! Yes!!!

My prayers join the author's, that you, dear reader, will read the book, study the Scripture presented, heed the testimonies and admonitions, and reap the benefits in your and other's lives! May God guide you as you read!

Rev. David E. Strong
Wilmington, New York

1

MY DILEMMA

"My people are destroyed for lack of knowledge."
(Hosea 4:6)

Joe was a friend, a big powerful man who had been an All-American football tackle. He was also a very successful evangelist who was being mightily used by the Lord. He had held several revivals for me through the years in various churches that I pastored. I always looked forward to Joe being with us. He was a very kind, helpful, spiritual man with whom I enjoyed good fellowship.

In a message to the church during one of these revivals, Joe said, "I believe that over 90% of all sickness among Christians is because of sin!" Being a young, impressionable preacher, I too, while preaching, would on occasion say, "I believe that over 90% of all sickness among Christians is because of sin!"

We kept in touch through the years. Not many years later I received a letter from Joe requesting prayer. His need...he had suffered a heart attack and was laid aside in a hospital bed unable to preach scheduled revivals. Being a very well-known evangelist in great demand, he usually stayed fully booked for years in advance. Along with his letter, Joe had included a photograph of himself lying in the hospital bed.

After I had read the letter and looked at the photo, my first reaction was..."Could this heart attack be because of sin?" "Had Joe fallen out of favor with

God?" This physical problem my Christian brother was experiencing troubled me greatly, because I knew what a great work he had been doing for the Lord. Also, we had prayed together on many occasions, and I knew of his total commitment to the work of the Lord and the many personal sacrifices he was making in his dedication to full-time evangelism.

CHRISTIAN LEADER SUFFERS STROKE

Then it happened again not too many years later to another Christian leader for whom I had the utmost respect; a man among men. This outstanding Christian, who was also an evangelist and the founder of a large Christian youth camp, experienced a stroke that left him partially paralyzed.

Christians all over the world were asked to pray, but his ministry was curtailed sharply and after several additional strokes, he died. Could these strokes and the untimely death of this great Christian leader be the result of sin??? Was his death the will of God??? It seems the stock answer among Christians when something like this happens is often, "It must have been God's will."

CHRISTIAN PUBLISHER HAS HEART ATTACK

Shortly thereafter, another evangelist, and publisher of a great Christian periodical that boldly stood for the fundamentals of the faith, suffered a heart attack. Christians and churches from all over the world once again were asked to pray, but after a continuing deterioration in his health, he also died. Was his death because of sin??? Could it be, that the death of this greatly used man of God was the will of God???

FOUNDER OF CHRISTIAN COLLEGE
SUFFERS FROM SENILITY

At about the same time another Christian leader, also an evangelist and the founder of one of the best-known Christian universities in America, was having a terrible problem with senility. His senility was so severe that for many years before his death he was unable to function or have any kind of ministry. Could his senility be the result of sin??? Could it be that this senility was the will of God???

By this time, I was extremely troubled at what I was seeing happen to men I respected; men I looked up to as the greatest spiritual leaders of the day. God had even used some of these men when He called me into the ministry.

CHRISTIAN MISSIONARY DIES FROM CANCER

Of all the troubling experiences I went through, the most upsetting up to this time, was something that happened at a preacher's conference around the year 1974. The church I was pastoring had been kind enough to send me to the conference for rest and refreshing. It was a time to fellowship with other preachers and to get my spiritual batteries recharged. However, I returned from this conference more perplexed and troubled than ever.

There were over 1200 preachers from all over the world attending this conference. Toward the end of the conference, the host pastor presented a missionary pastor to the gathered preachers. He was pastoring a church of some 15,000 people in the Philippines and was experiencing fantastic blessings in his ministry. However, he had been forced to leave this ministry because of cancer. At only 45 years of age, the doctors had given him only a few months to live.

We had special prayer for him. Over 1,200 preachers prayed for his healing. After we had collective prayer, we were encouraged to take this prayer request back to our respective churches and ask the people in our churches also to pray for his healing. This represented a potential in excess of 100,000 Christians praying for this evangelist to get well and be able to return to the field where he was doing such a mighty work for the

Lord.....But he did not get well.....In fact, he died not very long thereafter. Could his death have been the result of sin??? If his death was not because of sin, then why didn't the Lord answer the prayers of this multitude of Christians who were praying for his healing??? Was his death the will of God??? These were hard questions and they bothered me greatly as there just did not seem to be any answer that made sense. These were questions that I, as a pastor, felt I should know the answers to...but I didn't!!!

I am sharing only some of the most outstanding examples because all during these years I was seeing just ordinary, lesser-known Christians, as well as members of the various churches I was pastoring, experiencing numerous physical problems and seemingly untimely deaths. Many of my preacher friends also had physical ailments as well...some that were serious enough to hinder their ministries. Some of them had even died!

NOW IT WAS MY TURN

It was in 1976 however, that this whole perplexing problem of sickness among Christians came to a climax. Six years earlier I had started a new church in upstate New York. The church had grown from just my own family in the beginning to a membership of over 600. Some were driving in excess of 100 miles to attend our services. Many were coming to know the Lord Jesus as their personal Saviour.

We were broadcasting on three radio stations each week, and had five large buses on the road bringing people to Sunday School and church services. There was a printing ministry and a bookstore ministry. Our Christian school had over 100 students in grades kindergarten thru grade 12, along with a Bible Institute. Our Christian School was ranked as one of the top five Christian schools in the nation. Over a dozen of our young people were in Christian colleges, some preparing for full-time Christian work. None could deny that the Lord's blessing was on this ministry.

Then it happened! With all of these wonderful blessings going on in my own ministry, in 1976, at the age of 42, I was told that I had colon cancer, along with some other serious physical problems. Wow! This was mind-boggling! Could this sickness be because of "sin" in my own life??? Was this the will of God for me??? As I look back on it even to this day, I don't know how I could have been more sincere or dedicated to the Lord and His work. To say the least, this was all very devastating to me.

This all happened only a short time after I had watched my own mother die as a result of cancer following many years of medical treatment. Her illness and deterioration was a terrible thing to have to witness. I believe Mom suffered more from the treatments she received than she did from the cancer itself.

After watching my own mother go through this terrible ordeal, I was determined not to follow the conventional cancer treatments in my own body. So I searched for and found an alternative.....nutrition and a changed life style! It had worked for others, but there was no assurance that it would work for me. However, I felt it was at least an alternative that made sense and that did not contradict the teaching of the Bible, as did the administering of drugs.

I LEAVE THE MINISTRY

So I left the ministry and moved to a small town in Florida. There, I attended classes at a nutritional institute, as well as, put into practice the things that were being taught. Almost immediately unbelievable things started to happen in my body. Not only did the serious problems start to go away but even minor problems started to make their exit from my body as well. To say the least, it was very, very exciting. But I will talk more about this in a later chapter.

MY DILEMMA

Even more exciting than the healing I was experiencing in my own body was what I saw happening in the lives of others who were also at this nutritional institute. People were there from all over the world with all kinds of physical complaints. Many of these people were not professing Christians. Some of them were openly agnostics. Yet, when they applied the principles that were being taught.....truly miraculous healing took place and they got well.

Now I was really faced with a dilemma. For nearly 20 years while in the Christian ministry, I watched Christians get sick and often die from a variety of illnesses in spite of many prayers and the efforts of the medical profession. Now I was faced with personally witnessing even non-Christians getting well without prayer, the medical profession or even acknowledging God in their lives. How was I to account for this??? The rest of this book, **"Why Christians Get Sick"**, is devoted to answering this most important question.

CHAPTER ONE — IN REVIEW

Before we continue, let us think about this subject of sickness among Christians and ask some questions to stimulate our thinking:

1. Could it be possible that Christians are too passive when it comes to sickness, accepting and enduring sickness without resistance?

2. Could the reason for Christian passiveness be because we are fatalistic in our thinking? Webster defines fatalistic as: "that events are fixed in advance for all time in such a manner that human beings are powerless to change them."

3. Could it be possible that we are attributing sickness to "sin", or "the will of God" when, in reality the cause of that sickness might be the violation of some natural laws of God?

4. Have YOU ever wondered why Christians are just

as sick as non-Christians?   Or why spiritual
Christians are just as sick as Christians that
are not as spiritual?

5. Could it be possible that Christians don't have
to experience heart attacks, strokes, cancer,
senility, diabetes, and a host of other ailments
including colds, flu, headaches, sinuses, allergies,
pimples, tooth decay, arthritis, etc.???

6. Could it be that Christians don't want to acknowledge the possibility that perhaps something
they are doing (or not doing) is responsible for
their illness???   (Blaming instead some outside
force, such as germs, heredity, viruses, fate, God,
etc.)

7. Could it be possible that Christians are getting
sick and dying untimely deaths because *"My
people are destroyed for lack of knowledge"???*
(Hosea 4:6)

2

I AM FEARFULLY AND WONDERFULLY MADE

"I will praise thee; for I am fearfully and wonderfully made: marvelous are thy works; and that my soul knoweth right well."

(Psalm 139:14)

I believe that God created man!!! I do not believe that man's existence is the result of some evolutionary process!!! For just as a watch, which is so intricately made, must have a watch maker, man, who is so much more intricately made, had to have a Maker!!!

I also believe that the Bible is the very "Word of God"; that God not only created man, but also had a book of instructions written — *"All scripture is given by inspiration of God, and is profitable..."* (II Timothy 3:16). This book of instructions, the Bible, contains all that God the Creator, wanted man, His creation, to know!!! Yea, all that men needed to know in order to live a healthy, happy, successful, spiritual life is found in the pages of the Bible!!!

The Bible answers the three basic questions of man. Namely: "Where did man come from?", "Why is he here?", and "Where is he going when his life here on earth is over?" In this chapter, we must lay some ground work, so that in later chapters we may fully understand **"Why Christians Get Sick."**

WHERE DID MAN COME FROM

The Bible says, *"In the beginning, God created the heaven and the earth."* (Genesis 1:1) Then the Bible goes on in Genesis Chapter 1, to explain the six days of creation.

DAY ONE — GOD CREATED LIGHT (Genesis 1:3-5)
DAY TWO — GOD CREATED VAPOR ABOVE,
    WATER BELOW (Genesis 1:6-8)
DAY THREE — GOD CREATED LAND, SEA AND
    PLANT LIFE (Genesis 1:9-13)
DAY FOUR — GOD CREATED SUN, MOON
    AND STARS (Genesis 1:14-19)
DAY FIVE — GOD CREATED ANIMAL
    LIFE (Genesis 1:20-23)
DAY SIX — GOD CREATED CATTLE AND
    MAN (Genesis 1:24-31)

Let's examine the sixth day of creation more carefully, as it is extremely relevant to the understanding of **"Why Christians Get Sick?"**

First, let's see how the Bible says that God made man.....*"And the Lord God formed man of the Dust of the Ground, and breathed into his nostrils the breath of life: And man became a living soul."* (Genesis 2:7)

When the Bible states, *"I am fearfully and wonderfully made",* truer words were never spoken. Our body is literally a chemical factory, composed of almost every element in the mineral kingdom. Listing only the major elements, man is composed of: oxygen (68%), carbon (15%), hydrogen (10%), nitrogen (3%), calcium (2%) phosphorus (1%), along with trace amounts of sulfur, sodium, chlorine, flourine, potassium, magnesium, iron, silicon, iodine, copper, lead, aluminum, etc.

From the above, it is clear to see that man is made up primarily of the airborn elements ("Breath of Life"), approximately 96%, while the remaining elements come from the earth ("Dust of the Ground") about 4%. The Bible repeatedly confirms that God used these building materials in the making of man: *"In the sweat of thy face shalt thou eat bread, till thou return unto the ground; for out of it was thou taken: for dust thou art, and unto dust shalt thou return."* (Genesis 3:19) See also Psalm 103:14 and Ecclesiastes 12:7.

So, here we have a Book, written thousands of years ago, telling us the building material of which man is made: "The Dust of the Ground" and "The Breath of Life." These statements of the Bible are confirmed by the most modern of scientific findings.....that man is indeed made of the elements contained in the earth and air. How can anyone doubt the Bible being anything but the very "Word of God"? Science has only recently discovered what the Bible has been telling us for milleniums!!!

125 TRILLION CELLS

This body of ours consists of about 125,000,000,000, 000 (125 trillion) cells, which require constant nourishment for rebuilding. These cells also require constant cleansing of contaminants. Some parts of the body are renewed as often as every week or so; much of the body is rebuilt every year; while the bones (or the skeleton) require as much as several years for total rebuilding and replacement.

If these cells are not provided with the proper building materials, and the cells are not kept cleansed of toxic material, progressively weaker cells will replace the strong cells with which we were born. These weaker cells eventually result in sickness, tooth decay, poor eye sight, loss of hearing, baldness, senility, cancer, as well as a host of other physical problems, and ultimately an early or untimely death.

When people start to experience these and other breakdowns in their bodies, they usually attribute the breakdown to heredity, getting older, or often in the case of many Christians..."the will of God". They never seem to realize that these problems are the direct result of failing to provide the body cells with

proper and adequate nourishment. Proper nourishment is absolutely essential for the replenishment
of the cells, so that new cells will be as strong or stronger than those they are replacing.

Nor do people realize that their life-style and diets
have polluted their bodies.....bodies so full of poisons
that the cells are literally being drowned in these
pollutants. Thus we see that the health and condition
of the cells determines the health and condition of the
entire body.

THE BLOOD

The human body, depending on size, has approximately five quarts of blood which are constantly
traveling through the entire body, making 3,000 to
5,000 round trips a day! The heart pumps some
20,000,000,000 (20 billion) blood cells throughout the
body. These blood cells carry nourishment to the body
cells, while collecting wastes to be removed from the
body.

The heart muscle must be kept strong in order to keep
the blood continuously moving with good strength as
it feeds and cleanses the body cells. Many people fail
to realize the absolute necessity of aerobic exercises
for the maintaining of a strong heart to pump the
blood.

THE LUNGS

The respiratory system (lungs) works together with
the circulatory system (heart, arteries, veins, and
blood) as the life support system of the body. The body
can go 40 plus days without food, possibly 4 days
without water, but less than 4 minutes without air
(oxygen).

The lungs take in oxygen and give off carbon dioxide. The oxygen is picked up by the blood and taken to
every part of the body where it becomes food for the
building of new cells. On its return trip, it picks up
the garbage.....carbon dioxide and other toxins and

returns them to the lungs for removal from the body.

It is carbon dioxide that causes soda pop to bubble and fizz. When a person drinks a carbonated drink, little do they realize that they are dumping a toxic substance into their body.

If the oxygen supply is restricted by a clogged artery to the brain, a stroke results. If that restriction is to the heart, a heart attack is the result. Our life-style and diet determine the condition of our lungs, arteries, veins, etc., and the availability of oxygen to the cells.

The breathing of polluted air and smoking are like committing slow suicide! Every breath of these pollutants shortens the life of that individual.

THE LIVER

The liver takes every particle of food we eat and everthing we drink into its marvelous laboratory and breaks it down into a useable form. The blood then takes this specially prepared food to the various parts of the body to repair, replenish, and rebuild cells and tissues.

Alcohol, beer, wine, and liquor slowly destroy this marvelous organ which ultimately results in serious physical problems and untimely deaths.

OTHER ORGANS

If space permitted, we could talk about the lymph (which we will cover in a later chapter), nerves, muscles, glands, and a host of other parts with which God made man. But, I believe we have already shown more than enough to prove the Bible accurate when it states *"We are fearfully and wonderfully made."*

CHAPTER TWO — IN REVIEW

At the conclusion of each chapter, we will review some of the most important things we have learned:

1. God made man from the elements found in the dust and in the air!
2. Scientific evidence confirms that man's body is indeed comprised of the elements found in soil and air.
3. The body consists of trillions of cells which are in a constant state of being replaced.
4. Proper building materials are absolutely necessary for the building of strong, healthy, vibrant cells.
5. The blood constantly transports these building materials from the liver and lungs to every part of the body.
6. If any part of the body lacks health and efficient function, it is because the building materials brought by the blood has been unsuitable or inadequate for the purpose of maintaining health, and/or the body is polluted with poisons.
7. The only source from which the blood can derive the building materials for the re-building of cells is from the food we eat, the liquid we drink, and the air we breath.

3

BIBLICAL REASONS

"For this cause many are weak and sickly among you, and many sleep."

(I Corinthians 11:30)

Have you ever wondered, "Why Christians are just as sick as non-Christians???" Or, "Why spiritual Christians are just as sick as Christians that are not as spiritual???" These two questions were asked at the conclusion of Chapter One of this book. But they are two questions that greatly bothered me during many years while pastoring various churches.

As we saw in Chapter One, I have seen great Christian leaders.....evangelists, missionaries, and pastors.....get sick and even die, some in the prime of life doing great works for the Lord. I have also seen Christians get cancer, have heart attacks, strokes, diabetes, arthritis, flu, headaches, colds, upset stomachs, and you name it....just like non-Christians. As Christians, how can we account for this???

WHAT VARIOUS RELIGIONS TEACH

Different religions have had some very interesting teachings and practices concerning sickness. Let's look at some of them:

CHRISTIAN SCIENCE, founded by Mary Baker Glover Patterson Eddy, teaches that sickness and death are not real, only mental error. Yet the founder of this religion, as well as multitudes of its followers (including one of my own aunts who was a Christian Scientist), got sick and died.

SEVENTH DAY ADVENTISTS, founded by Ellen G. White, have included in the teachings of their religion some very strict teachings on diet and care of the body. For instance, they teach against the use of coffee, tea, tobacco, and alcoholic beverages. One of the more interesting teachings is that they are to eat no pork and that it is best to eat no meat at all. Though the followers of this religion have not all followed these dietary teachings, statistics show that Adventists have less incidence of cancer and in general are healthier than the average American. Further, as a group, they live six years longer than the average American.

MORMONS, founded by Joseph Smith, also include in their teachings, dietary restrictions. These include abstaining from the use of alcohol, tobacco, coffee, tea, cola, and any other substance containing a drug. They also encourage the storage of emergency food..... especially grains and pure drinking water.

PENTECOSTALS, generally teach that healing of the body was included in the atonement. They often have healing services and healing lines at which time they may apply oil along with prayers for healing. I have personally been in meetings where they demanded God to heal the affliction in the "Name of Jesus." But in some 20 years of ministry, coming in contact with many Pentecostal pastors and their parishioners, I have not seen any less frequency of sickness among this group.

PROTESTANTS, CATHOLICS AND JEWS, seem to view sickness in general as some kind of judgement upon them by God. Often, they view sickness and death as something that just has to be accepted, and that they are powerless to change their fate. If prayer or the medical profession doesn't bring relief, then it must be "God's will."

BAPTISTS, (and I was a Baptist pastor for almost 20 years) are often extremely fatalistic when it comes to sickness. They pray very sincerely and they accept treatment with drugs, radiation and surgery by the medical profession as a means that God uses to heal Christians who are sick. If prayers and the efforts of the medical profession don't bring healing, then that sickness is accepted as the "Will of God." But in over 30 years of association with Baptists, I have not seen them, as a group, to have any better health than non-Baptists.

IS GOD TO BLAME?

I have not included the above review for the purpose of being unkind. However, I believe that it is high time we stopped hiding behind the Lord and blaming Him for our physical problems. And that is exactly what we are doing most of the time when we say "It's God Will" when sickness comes to us, a friend, or one of our loved ones.

It seems that we tend to blame things we do not understand on the Lord. For instance: A tornado devastates a town in Oklahoma; or a hurricane rips the coast of Louisiana; or floods inundate a certain community. In each of these incidents, human lives are lost and there is great property damage. Who gets the blame for these tragedies? Why, "It was an act of God" according to the insurance company or the news commentator. What they are actually saying is, "God's to blame!"

Let's stop blaming God for things we don't understand! And let's turn to the BIBLE, and see what the Lord has to tell us about this subject of sickness among Christians.....just why do Christians get sick???

The Bible gives only three reasons for sickness or physical problems among Christians, and I believe that every physical affliction suffered by Christians today, falls into one of these three categories.

I. FOR THE GLORY OF GOD

In the Gospel of John, Chapter 9, verses 1-3, we read of a man who was blind from birth. Neither he nor his parents had sinned. The Bible asks: *Who did sin, this man or his parents, that he was born blind?"* Jesus answered, *"Neither hath this man sinned, nor his parents, but that the works of God should be made manifest in him."*

It is very clear that this incident happened while Jesus was on this earth and that this blindness was for a purpose....so that Jesus could heal him, thus calling attention to Himself, who He was, and to the Father who sent Him!

The Apostle Paul seemed to have a physical affliction that would fit into this category. Paul prayed three times for healing but the Lord said in II Corinthians 12:7-9: *".....My grace is sufficient for thee."*

If this is our lot, and we have a sickness for the glory of God, then we must learn to say as Paul did, *"For I have learned, that in whatsoever state I am, therewith to be content."* (Philippians 4:11) All the praying in the world will not remove an affliction that is for the glory of God.

II. BECAUSE OF UNCONFESSED SIN

In I Corinthians 11:28-32 we read about weakness, sickness and an early death coming upon believers when they would not confess their sins, and God had to judge them. *"For this cause many are weak and sickly among you, and many sleep. For if we would judge ourselves, we should not be judged. But when we are judged, we are chastened of the Lord, that we should not be condemned with the world."* (II Corinthians 11:30-32)

According to the Bible, *Some Christians do suffer physical afflictions because of sin!* However, this affliction can be quickly remedied by carrying out the teachings of I John 1:9: *"If we confess our sins, he is faithful and just to forgive us our sins and to cleanse us from all unrighteousness."*

Sickness because of sin is a judgement by the Lord, but it can be removed if we make things right with the Lord. Re-read I Corinthians 11:30-32 in this regard. And by the way, all the praying in the world will not heal the affliction caused by sin, unless it is the prayer of repentence by the believer who has sinned!

I have no doubt that some of the physical suffering among Christians of our day is because of unconfessed sin. However, I believe that the physical sufferings of this group comprises a very small percentage of today's physical problems.

Today, if a Christian is experiencing a physical problem, it is easy enough to find out if the sickness is because of sin.....sincerely confess all known sin and ask the Lord's forgiveness (I John 9). If this doesn't bring healing, then the sickness is almost certainly due to the third reason the Bible gives for sickness.....the violation of God's natural laws!

III. THE VIOLATION OF GOD'S NATURAL LAWS

In I Corinthians 3:16-18 we read, *"Know ye not that ye are the temple of God and that the spirit of God dwelleth in you? If any man defile the temple of God, him shall God destroy: For the temple of God is holy, which temple ye are."*

These scriptures puzzled me for many years. It was not until I personally had physical problems, which resulted in my studying how the body functions and in learning the importance of proper nutrition and vigorous exercise, that my eyes were opened to what the Bible was teaching here in I Corinthians 3:16-18.

There is additional teaching on this subject in I Corinthians 6:19-20: *"What, know ye not that your body is the temple of the Holy Ghost which is in you, which ye have of God, and ye are not your own? For ye are bought with a price: therefore glorify God in your body, and in your spirit, which are God's."*

Clearly, the Bible teaches that the *Christian's body is not his own.....it belongs to God!!!* If a Christian fails to care properly for his body, *God will destroy that body!!!* Let's read that scripture again....."*If any man defile* ('make unclean with something unpleasant or contaminating' Webster) *the temple of God, him shall God destroy.*" (I Corinthians 3:17)

OUR LACK OF KNOWLEDGE

Most people never give a second thought as to what they put into their mouth. If it tastes good, they eat it. They never seem to associate their physical condition with what they eat or drink. If people were to read the ingredients on the labels before putting things into their mouths, they would be amazed at what they are consuming....substances they often can't even pronounce, much less know what they are! The average person uses more care in selecting the grade of gasoline to put into their automobiles than they do the food they put in their mouth.

Nor do people normally associate the exercise their body receives (or fails to receive) as having anything to do with their physical health. The Bible says we are *"Destroyed for lack of knowledge."* (Hosea 4:6)

PURPOSE FOR WRITING BOOK

My purpose in writing this book, is to share with you my Christian brother or sister, some of the knowledge I have obtained and experienced, concerning the body and health. Knowledge that, when applied, has literally changed my body and life.....feeling as good or better than I did when I was 20 years old.

Some will heed this knowledge and see marvelous things start to happen within their own bodies. Health will be their portion, and life will take on a new glow. Just feeling so alive will excite you, and living for Jesus will become an increasingly thrilling experience!

Others will reject this knowledge and go on their merry, miserable way to a diseased body, much suffering, and a premature death. *"Be not deceived; God is not mocked: Whatsoever a man soweth, that shall he also reap."* (Galatians 6:7) This scripture most certainly applies to the subject we have been discussing; **"Why Christians Get Sick."**

Then there may be someone who says, "But I would rather go to be with Jesus.....this world is so wicked, and being with Jesus will be so wonderful, and besides, I'll have a new body." Oh, but you can have a new body here and now if you want it!!! And let's remember the Apostle Paul's words: *"For I am in a straight betwixt two, having a desire to depart, and to be with Christ; which is far better: Nevertheless to abide in the flesh is more needful for you."* (Philippians 1:23-24)

CHAPTER THREE — IN REVIEW

1. Christians are just as sick as non-Christians. Spiritual Christians are just as sick as Christians who are not as spiritual. WHY???

2. Christians tend to be very fatalistic in their view of sickness, often attributing to, or even blaming, God for their physical problems.

3. The Bible teaches only three reasons for sickness among Christians:

   I - FOR THE GLORY OF GOD...primarily used in Biblical days to demonstrate the Lord Jesus Christ's power and deity.

   II - BECAUSE OF UNCONFESSED SIN by the Christian. Some of the sickness among Christians today, can no doubt, be attributed to this cause. Repentant prayer will bring healing in this instance.

   III - THE VIOLATION OF THE NATURAL LAWS OF GOD. It is in this third category that the author believes we will find the cause for over 90% of all Christian sickness and physical suffering being experienced today.

4. Our poor eating habits, life style, and lack of

exercise cause most of our physical problems.
5. We do have a choice!!! Will it be health and happiness or sickness, suffering and an untimely death??? Which will you choose???

4

TRADITIONAL REASONS

"Beware lest any man spoil you through.....the traditions of men."

(Colossians 2:8)

The lack of knowledge in a particular subject can be devastating.....so much so that the Bible says in Hosea 4:6; *"My people are destroyed for lack of knowledge."*

This scripture was used at the beginning of Chapter One where we saw a number of prominent Christians having serious physical problems and untimely deaths. If Christians are having physical problems and experiencing early deaths because of lack of knowledge, this becomes a very serious and tragic matter indeed!!! For a few moments, let us consider the word **"Knowledge"**, especially as it pertains to Christians.

THE IMPORTANCE OF KNOWLEDGE

Christians are a very unique group of people. They have personally gained **knowledge** in spiritual matters, resulting in the receiving of Jesus as Saviour. This knowledge and the applying of this knowledge brings a person out of spiritual darkness into God's marvelous light.

However, this spiritual knowledge which we have can lead us into trouble if we are not careful. Why???... Because we have come to know the truth in spiritual matters, we often think we know everything about everything, which results in our closing our minds to anything contrary to what we believe, no matter what the subject.

Knowledge is one of the greatest needs of Christians!!! Jesus spoke about it often. In John 8:32, Jesus said: *"And ye shall **know** the truth, and the truth shall make you free."* And again in John 13:17, *"If you **know** these things, happy are ye if ye do them."*

NEED FOR OPEN MINDS

Christians should have open minds, like the Berean Christians did in Acts 17. I'm not saying we should believe everything, but we should at least listen to it, and then see if it has any validity by checking it against the Word of God. Sadly though, many Christians close their minds to anything different from what their minds are programmed with.....often ignorant of the truth, foolishly substituting opinions, theories, traditions and blind beliefs for **true knowledge.**

Christians (as do non-Christians) often tie themselves to beliefs that were handed down from previous generations, or they hold prejudices picked up along their journey through life. Often these beliefs are false, but the mind is often closed to any other opinion. Thus, this closed mind becomes our greatest obstacle to gaining **knowledge** and **truth!** I have even seen Christians reject clear Bible teachings because of closed minds concerning a particular subject.

LACK OF **KNOWLEDGE** APPALLING

The lack of **knowledge** concerning **"Why Christians Get Sick"** is appalling, and I must admit, I was a star pupil in this ignorance for many, many years. My Christian brother or sister reading this book, will you open your mind enough to at least explore the subject before us??? I am not asking you to accept blindly what I'm saying in this book...but what I am asking is that you be as open minded as the Berean Christians of Acts 17:11 who *"Received the word with all readiness of mind, and searched the scriptures daily whether those things were so."* Will you at least allow your mind to explore the subject? You have nothing to lose except possibly some false beliefs and you might just swap that old belief for a long, healthy, excitingly productive Christian life!!!

In order to gain **knowledge,** we need to begin by separating what we know to be true, from what we have always accepted. We need to separate **true knowledge** from beliefs or opinions.

TRADITIONS

Let's ask a few questions to stimulate our thinking: "Why do you eat the way you do...Why do you use a fork and spoon, instead of chop sticks or some other instrument to place food into your mouth?" "Why do most Americans eat three major meals a day, while in other parts of the world two and sometimes only one is the norm?" "Why is the majority of food that is consumed in America, cooked?" "Why do many people not consider a meal complete without a sugar dessert?"

I don't think it is necessary to ask any more questions because the answer will probably be the same to them all: "That's just the way I was brought up." Thus we see, that tradition has played a great part in determining what we put into our body, and the manner in which it is consumed.

EATING HABITS HANDED DOWN

Most Christians, like myself, were brought up to eat like their parents before them. Not that our parents meant us any harm; it's just that eating habits tend to be handed down from one generation to the next.

For instance, when I was pastoring a church in eastern North Carolina some years ago, pork was consumed in large quantities. In fact, most meals contained two (and sometimes three) different meats, and almost every vegetable dish was prepared with a large piece of "fat back" (the traditional way of eating in the area). Because of these traditional eating habits, there was an extremely high rate of circulatory problems and early deaths caused by clogged arteries.

Tradition plays an extremely large part in the way we eat, what we eat, and the physical problems that we experience!

MOM DIES AFTER BOUT WITH CANCER

My mother died after a horrible experience with colon cancer. At the age of 42, I was told that I had cancer of the colon. Did that mean that I had an inherent weakness that was passed on to me by my mother (which is strongly taught by many medical authorities)? Or could it be that the way my mom and I ate, and the things we ate, and the way that we lived were similar enough to produce similar physical problems?

DAD DIES FROM HEART ATTACK

My dad had numerous heart attacks and strokes, starting at the age of 42...finally dying from one of these heart attacks. When I was 42 years old, the doctor told me that my body was ripe for a heart attack or stroke. Had I inherited a weak heart and circulation system from my dad? Or could it be that dad and I both had eaten a similar diet, prepared in a similar manner along with a similar life style?

HOW I RESPONDED TO PERSONAL PHYSICAL PROBLEMS

How was I to respond to these physical problems that I was experiencing in my own body? I could have said, "Well, it must be God's will for my life," and just done nothing. Or I could have placed myself in the hands of medical doctors who were unable to help either mother or dad. Or thirdly, I could set out on a quest for **knowledge,** to find out why my body was experiencing these problems, and seek to find a solution. As I stated in Chapter One, I chose the third option and ultimately changed my diet and life-style, and started doing vigorous exercising, along with some other changes.

HOW MY BODY RESPONDED

How did my body respond to these changes? Well, let's see how my heart and circulatory system reacted. In 1976, at the age of 42, my blood pressure was normally around 150/90, which is considered borderline high blood pressure. Six years later, at the age of 48, after changing my diet and becoming physically active, my blood pressure was down to 125/75. Today, at age 59, seventeen years after I was told my body was ripe for a heart attack or stroke, my blood pressure runs around 110/70.

At age 42, my pulse rate at rest was in the lower 70's. Today, at the age of 59, my pulse rate at rest is in the upper 40's. Even after jogging five miles in less than an hour, my pulse rate is under 120.

Now I ask you a question: "Would you say that my physical problems at the age of 42 were (a) the "Will of God", (b) weaknesses inherited from my parents, or (c) the results of tradition? Or possibly the result of a combination of two causes, tradition and altered tradition?

ALTERED TRADITION

The traditional eating habits of most Americans have been altered by the strong advertising of today's food merchants, the fast food craze, and a faster pace of life. Let's explore altered tradition with another personal illustration.

My mother's parents, my grandparents, were both hard working farm people...out in the fields at the crack of dawn, living a simple life of hard work and eating primarily simple meals prepared from the food raised in their own gardens and orchard. They didn't even have electricity or running water. Yet, both remained strong and active into their 80's.

From this strong stock, their daughter, my mother, was in serious physical trouble before the age of 50. Then her son, yours truly, was in serious physical trouble by the age of 42. You can clearly see the downward progression of health from one generation to the next.

Does altered tradition have anything to do with **"Why Christians Get Sick?"** Let's explore this thought, and when I talk about altered tradition, I'm talking about a change from the way our ancestors grew, processed, prepared and consumed their food in comparison to today.

CHEMICALS

For instance, prior to World War II, there was very little use of insecticides (chemical poisons) used in the growing of food. Today, over 1,000,000,000 (one billion) pounds of insecticides are sprayed or dusted on the foods Americans consume each year. (Incidently, less than 1% of that billion pounds of insecticide ever reaches the insect it was intended to destroy).

In the early days of insecticides, you could at least wash off the poison or remove the poison by peeling the fruit or vegetable. Today, there are systemic poisons that are taken in by the plant and become an integral part of the plant. Thus, the poison is on the inside and impossible to remove.

I've just talked about the insecticides. In the raising of our food today, also used are herbicides (poisons) to kill weeds, and fungicides to destroy fungi or inhibit their growth. Unless you have your own garden, or have access to produce raised on an organic farm, it is impossible to escape these poisons.

"Pesticides can damage and tax your immune

system at the same time. The damage can be both acute and cumulative. Since many toxic chemicals are stored in your fat cells and lymph glands, they can remain in the body for decades. Thus, health problems can build up over a long period in ways that science doesn't yet fully understand. One of the most dangerous effects of pesticides is that they weaken your immune system so you are less able to combat even ordinary infections. Symptoms of a weakened immune system might include: skin rashes, nausea, fatigue, depression, leukemia, frequent infections, and fever." (**Organic Gardening** magazine, April 1988, page 59)

PRESERVATIVES

When our grandparents were growing up, the only preservatives used in foods were salt and vinegar. Today, with modern processing, it is hard to find a prepared food that doesn't contain chemical preservatives, along with artificial colorings, artificial flavorings, stabilizers, emulsifiers, and so forth.

Most of the additives that have been tested have been proven to cause harmful effects on the test animals...yet the average American consumes over seven pounds of these poisons annually. There are literally thousands of different toxic chemicals being used on our foods today: BHA, BHT, sodium nitrate, sodium nitrite, calcium propionate, EDTA, red dyes, yellow dyes, and the list goes on and on and on. Let's look at just one example:

Beatrice Hunter, in her book **"Food Additives and Your Health"**, states on pages 47-48 "...severe allergic reactions have been reported for BHT (and BHA), including "debilitating and disabling chronic asthmatic attacks," skin blistering, eye hemorrhaging, tingling sensations on face and hands, extreme weakness, fatigue, edema, chest tightness and difficulty in breathing."

There is no such thing as a **safe** chemical!!! All

chemicals are toxic to the body and produce adverse reactions within the body!!!

Most Americans just take it for granted that if it is a product sold for food, that it is safe to eat. NOT SO!!! It's also amazing, but true, that the average person never associates his physical problems with what he eats or drinks.

WATER

Our ancestors drank water from a well or spring that was basically pure. The water most people drink today comes from a municipal water supply that has been chlorinated, fluoridated, and usually contains a host of impurities and toxic minerals.

Even most wells, and springs, have been contaminated by the pollution of our ground water from chemical poisons used in farming and from chemical spills and dumps. More about water in later chapters.

MILK

Milk is another example. As a child, I often visited my aunt and uncle's farm. After the morning milking, some of the fresh, warm milk was placed in a pitcher on the breakfast table within minutes after leaving the cow. This fresh milk received no processing!

Today, milk goes from the cow to bulk holding tanks for cooling. Then it is picked up by a tanker truck that hauls it to a processing plant. At the processing plant it is pasteurized...heated to a least 160 degrees to kill bacteria (the heating also destroys almost the total nutritional value of the milk). Then it is homogenized so that the cream won't rise to the top, and, finally coal-tar-derived vitamins are added in an attempt to replace some of the natural vitamins removed in processing. After processing, it is placed in plastic, waxed cardboard or, on occasion, glass containers and ultimately finds its way into the home and body.

We are told that milk is a great source of calcium. Yet most people are unaware that pasteurization (the heating process), renders the calcium unusable by the body. The reason?...Heat changes the organic calcium found in raw milk to an inorganic form. The body can only utilize organic minerals.

As a boy, I can remember having a terrible problem with cavities in my teeth. The dentist told my parents to increase the amount of milk I drank. My parents did just that, and I consumed large quantities of pasteurized milk. But instead of reducing the number of cavities, the number of cavities increased!

FLOUR

What have the processors done with whole wheat flour? Well, the first thing that they do is remove the germ, which contains most of the food value, because it gums up their machinery. Next, they remove the bran because it leaves brown specks in the flour. (By the way, both the wheat germ and the wheat bran are then sold back to the public in health food stores as health foods.)

They then take what is left after removing the germ and bran and bleach it (with chemical bleaching agents similar to clorox) to make it nice and white. Next, they add coal-tar-derived vitamins, package it, and sell it to the unsuspecting public as enriched bread.

That's sure a far cry from the way our ancestors made their flour. And can you imagine the nutritional value in today's baked products? Try reading the label on the next loaf of bread you buy.

OILS AND FATS

Other items that have been altered are oils and fats. In past generations, butter and lard were the leading oils and fats used in America. Butter was made from unpasteurized raw milk and usually no salt was added. Most people today realize that lard was and is a very harmful substance to the body.

Modern technology and processing has brought us a

substitute for butter that is usually less costly and often promoted as being better for you than butter... it is call margarine. Margarine is made by taking liquid oil, heating it to a high temperature and then bubbling hydrogen gas through it until it becomes hardened. Then it is bleached, filtered and deodorized, producing an odorless, taste-less, artificial fat!

This process changes a poly-unsaturated oil into a TOTALLY SATURATED FAT!!! The kind that causes high cholesterol problems...clogs the arteries which ultimately results in heart attacks, strokes and cancer. The ultimate product is a substance very similar to lard. A substance the body has no means of digesting!

Besides being used in margarine, hydrogenated oils and fat are used extensively in shortening, baked and fried products and most brands of peanut butter. Some nutritionists believe that margarine is the single most **dangerous** "so-called" food on the American market!!!

MEAT

Is meat being raised today, any different than it was in our grandparents' day? The answer to that question is "yes"! All sorts of drugs are being added to the animals' food and drink; like antibiotics to keep them well, and growth hormones to cause them to grow faster.

Chickens that lay eggs sold in the market usually never see the light of day. These animals are raised in wire cages where they can hardly move, so that all energy will go into egg production. Their food and water is brought to them automatically by conveyor. Various chemical substances, including antibiotics are added to feed and water.

This is certainly far removed from the back yard flock our ancestors kept, which were able to eat greens, bugs, worms as well as having sunlight and a rooster, each adding nutrition to the egg.

We could go on with many other illustrations, but I believe it is clear to any thinking person that there is hardly a single food in the marketplace today that hasn't been altered in some way from the way it was raised or prepared in past generations.

FAST FOODS

We are living in a day where the pace of life is too fast. Housewives are to busy to prepare meals in the traditional way. Fast food restaurants are on every corner. Micro-wave ovens and convenience foods are the norm.

Most women today feel that these convenience foods are a blessing, in that they require less time for pre-paration. But are they a blessing, or are they helping contribute to the multitude of physical problems plaguing the families of today?

I'll just give one example, which will hopefully help you to understand the hazards in convenience foods.....
All canned, bottled and most frozen fruit juices are heated to high temperatures so that they will have an extended shelf life without spoilage. Someone reading the preceding sentence might possibly say, "So what if these juices are heated with high heat... what's the big deal about that?"

To show why it is a "big deal" if you want to be physically strong and healthy, we will look more close-ly at just one juice...orange juice.

ORANGE JUICE

In order to make frozen orange juice into concen-trate, they first squeeze the juice from the orange. Next, the moisture content is removed either by boiling it away or by spray drying. Both methods use high heat to remove this moisture and produce an orange juice concentrate.

The concentrate is then frozen, and placed in storage until shipped to the wholesaler, and finally to the retailer. The consumer then purchases this frozen concentrate and re-constitutes it by replacing the liquid that had previously been removed from it. The water added is usually from a municipal water supply.

Here is the problem....when the orange juice was subjected to the high temperatures it lost more than the water content....it lost 100% of its enzymes, over 80% of the vitamins and 100% of the organic minerals that were in the fresh juice. In other words, the processing destroyed almost the entire nutritional value of the originally freshly squeezed juice. Also, the water added in re-constituting the juice was inferior to the liquid removed originally.

Today, we have been programmed to accept ease, speed and convenience....little realizing that each step of processing takes us further from the real thing!!

VITAMINS

"Vitamins", most of our ancestors would ask... "what are they?" The food merchants remove most of the nutrients in order to keep foods from spoiling, as we saw above. Then they often add various substances so that the food will taste better, look nicer, and smell good. Finally, they add preservatives so that the product will have a longer shelf life which increases sales and profits.

Then, after the nutrients are all but totally destroyed in processing, the food industry adds vitamins that will supposedly make up for the nutritional loss. Don't believe it!!! It just doesn't work that way!!! They cannot replace the nutrients that were originally in the whole living food with something dead and artificial!!!

GASOLINE

As I mentioned earlier in the book, it is probably not an exaggeration to say that most Christians are more concerned with the brand and grade of gasoline they put into their automobiles than they are about the quality and nutritional value of the food they put into their bodies.

This was true in my own life...not that I was intentionally trying to destroy myself, or that I didn't care about my body...I was just lacking in knowledge! I was really very ignorant concerning this subject. I was the victim of tradition and altered tradition. I contend that much of the sickness and physical problems among Christians today can be traced directly to this cause!!!

In the Bible, in Genesis 6:13, we see where God destroyed most of His creation because *"Man had corrupted God's way upon the earth."* Man had changed things from the way God intended them to be.

As far as the food we eat, we most certainly have changed it from the way our Creator made it and intended it to be. We poison it while it is growing, remove the nutrients in processing, add toxic substances to it, and then blame God when we get sick....may God help us!!!

CHAPTER FOUR — IN REVIEW

1. Christians are often lacking in KNOWLEDGE concerning the relationship between food, nutrition, lifestyle and health!
2. Many of our physical problems stem from our following the traditional methods of preparing and eating our foods!
3. Altered tradition has most certainly played its part by changing the food from the manner in which God intended it to be consumed.
4. Poisons are added to our food while it is being grown!
5. Poisons are added to our foods during processing!
6. Poisons are added to our drinking water!
7. Milk has most of its nutrients destroyed during processing!
8. During processing, flour not only has the nutrients removed, but then it is bleached and has artificial nutrients added!

9. Some nutritionists believe that margarine is the single most dangerous food on the American market!
10. Meat and eggs are tampered with!
11. Fast foods and convenience foods are usually far removed from the real thing!!!
12. Almost six thousand years ago, God destroyed most of His creation, because man had changed things from the way He intended them to be!

5

DRUGS AND THE MEDICAL PROFESSION

"And a certain woman, which had an issue of blood twelve years, and had suffered many things of many physicians, and had spent all that she had, and was nothing better, but rather grew worse."

(Mark 5:25-26)

Dan Rather, in a TV broadcast "CBS Reports", on January 10, 1975; said, "During 1974, Senate hearings under the chairmanship of Senator Edward Kennedy, focused on problems of drug use and safety." Senator Kennedy said, "This is a serious public health issue, and it's one that is generally not understood among the American people...and one that results in the death of, as we've heard estimated, anywhere from 40,000 to 120,000 deaths a year. We can't be specifically sure of the number. Some have said that it's a good deal higher...We've had estimates before our committee from responsible researchers that say the American consumer is paying $2,000,000,000 (two billion dollars) a year more than he should because of adverse drug reactions....."

My Christian friend, that was disclosed in 1974! Since then, the problem has grown much worse! And remember, we're talking about so-called legal drugs, prescribed by the medical profession.

THE MEDICINE MAN

In some parts of the world, people still believe disease and sickness is the work of an evil spirit. So when they become sick, they summon the "medicine man" or "witch doctor" who comes and prepares them a vile concoction, which they pour down their throats in hopes of making them well. We think of that as being very crude and primitive. But really now, have we advanced much further in this so-called "enlightened" generation???

Today when someone gets sick, he goes to a man (or woman) called a "medical doctor." This medical doctor, asks him what the problem is, often gives him some kind of an examination, and then, in language the person can't understand, writes something on a piece of paper (called a prescription). The sick person then takes that piece of paper to a drug store, where the druggest takes that piece of paper, mixes the potion prescribed (or reaches for the drug already mixed), puts it into a bottle, and the sick person pays the price. The sick person then takes this unknown substance (drug) into his body, hoping it will bring about relief from the symptoms. Talk about faith!!!

If the medical doctor can't find the drug that will relieve the symptoms, he sends the sick person home and classifies him as incurable or may suggest the problem is psychological. Have we really come as far as we think from the days of the "medicine man" and "witch doctor???"

WE LIVE IN A DRUG-ORIENTED SOCIETY

We live in a drug-oriented society! Our water is drugged with chlorine and fluoride (sodium fluoride). Chlorine is a bleaching agent. Sodium fluoride is used as a roach and rat poison. If there is enough chlorine in the water you drink so that you can smell it; there is enough chlorine to destroy the friendly bacteria in your intestinal tract and thus deprive the body of important vitamins these friendly bacteria manufacture for us, including vitamin B-12.

Our foods have been drugged with some 7,000 different chemicals (drugs) - sodium nitrite, sodium nitrate, BHA, BHT, EDTA, and a host of other preservatives (drugs), artificial flavorings (drugs), and colorings (drugs). About 1,000,000,000 (one billion) pounds of these drugs per year are consumed in America....that is over seven pounds for every man, woman and child every year!!!

Then, when we get sick from the drugs in our drinking water and from taking devitalized, drugged, so-called food substances into our body, we call the medical doctor. The medical doctor, a doctor licensed to practice the prescribing of drugs, writes a prescription for some more drugs, which is taken to the pharmacist ("one engaged in preparing, preserving, compounding and dispensing drugs," Webster). The pharmacist dispenses and sells the drugs. The sick person, whose sickness may quite possibly be a drug reaction from the drugged water and food, then takes these additional drugs, supposedly to cure his illness. How pathetic.....and we think we are so knowledgeable!!!

ASPIRIN

Every year, Americans consume over 16,000,000,000 (sixteen billion) aspirin. A drug that kills many persons legally each year! This is a non-prescription drug that has never cured anyone!!!

However, it does cover-up God's natural warning signal. For example, a headache is a warning signal, warning of an internal problem. How does the average American react to this warning signal? Why, he takes an aspirin or two, or three, and sometimes even more. What effect do these aspirin have on the body? They drug the body, thus relieving the pain, and short circuit the body's warning device.

How should we respond when we get a headache, or suffer from some other form of illness? Find the cause, eliminate the cause, and thus the headache or whatever the illness may be, will go away!!! And it will stay away as long as we stay away from what caused the headache or illness in the first place!!!

CHRISTIANS ARE DRUG ORIENTED

It is sad, but true, that Christians are just as drug oriented as non-Christians! If a Christian has a headache, he takes a drug, if he can't sleep, he takes a drug; if pregnancy is not desired, a drug is taken; if nervous, he takes a drug; drugs are even used to slow down an over-active child when the over-active child's problem is usually caused by the drugs he has been consuming in his food and drink.

Christians have been deceived into taking drugs because they are so widely used, advertised, and such an important part of the society in which we live. Often, Christians try to differentiate between "good" drugs and "bad" drugs.....probably because they do not understand what drugs are, what effect they have on the body, and what the Bible has to say about them!

WHAT IS A DRUG?

Wester's Dictionary defines a drug as "A substance other than food intended to affect the structure or function of the body."

As Christians, we need to realize that God is constantly warning against the use of all drugs and the deception of drugs. The Bible word for sorceries comes from the Greek word phar-ma-kia which today, in the English language, we call drugs. Revelation 18:23 says *"...for by sorceries (drugs) were all nations deceived."*

Today, most Christians have been deceived concerning drugs! They stand stongly and boldly against heroin, cocaine, crack, marijuana, and the like. Also, most Christians will not allow the drug of alcohol from beer, wine, and whiskey to enter their bodies. Most Christians refrain from the use of tobacco, and the drug, nicotine, isn't allowed to enter the body by way of smoking or chewing.

Why do Christians stand against these drugs? Because "these drugs are harmful and against God's will," we tell ourselves and our children. We also teach against these drugs in our Sunday School classes and preach against them from the pulpits of our churches.

And yet, Christians indulge in the taking of aspirin, sleeping pills, nerve pills, etc., and readily accept every pill and prescription the medical doctor prescribes without hesitation. My Christian friend, these are also drugs, and often just as harmful and contrary to the Word of God as is the cocaine, alcohol and nicotine that we condemn!!!

ALL DRUGS ARE FOREIGN SUBSTANCES AND POISONS TO THE BODY!!!

All drugs are toxic and have a poisoning effect on the body! God made a fantastic body, and He never intended these foreign substances (drugs) to enter it!!! But when they do enter the body, the body mobilizes its forces in an all out effort to remove these foreign, poisonous substances through every avenue at its disposal.

THE COMMON COLD

Take for example, the common cold, for which the medical profession has spent billions of tax-payers dollars trying to find the cause and cure but never has and never will!!! Why??? Because they are looking for a germ or virus....and that is the wrong place to look!

A cold is nothing more than the all-wise, God created body making an effort to cleanse itself of an accumulation of toxic waste!!!

What has the medical establishment told us to do? Stop the cold symptoms!!!!" "Take some aspirin (drug) to take away the headache and possible fever." "Take a de-congestant or anti-histamine (drugs) to stop the nose from running." Thus the body is drugged! The headache (a warning signal) goes away! The runny nose (which was removing copious amounts of poisons from the body) dries up! The person says, "Praise the Lord, my cold is gone!"

But what that person doesn't realize is that the poisons which were trying to make their way out of the body are **still in the body**, and will try again. The next time, it might be another "cold," or maybe next time it will be something more serious, like cancer!!!

Most Christians would not deliberately or knowingly try to poison their own bodies. But when that poison (drug) is called "medicine" they readily accept it as something that is all right to put into the body, no matter how vile it tastes or how violently the body reacts against it.

Only children seem to have enough sense to reject it. They often have to be forced into taking medicine or have it sugar coated (another drug) to make it palatable!

THE RESULTS

What has been the result of the mass drugging of the American population, including Christians??? **Rodale Press** has published figures to show that at least 200,000 Americans die annually at the hands of doctors! **The National Enquirer** states that 4,500,000 people each year are poisoned (drugged) so seriously by their physicians that they require hospitalization!

Over 40,000 die of this form of doctoring each year, and many believe this number exceeds 120,000 according to the Dan Rather report at the beginning of this chapter.

Remember, all drugs or medicines are inherently poisonous, and side effects or adverse reactions are just another way of saying poisonous effects or reactions!!

WE CANNOT BE DRUGGED INTO HEALTH

People cannot be drugged (poisoned) into health!!! Drugs create problems, rather than solve them!!! To regain health, the sick person must cleanse the body of the drugs and toxic substances that have accumulated and then provide the body with the proper building materials and influences that will allow the body to purify, repair and rebuild itself!!!

Health **cannot** be restored by taking drugs!!! Drugs **cannot** rebuild the cells of the body!!! The body is self-healing when healthful practices are followed!!! Just as you are able to witness the healing of a cut, covered by a scab, followed by new skin on the exterior as the body heals itself....just so it heals on the inside when conditions are made favorable for it to do so!!!

A DOCTOR SPEAKS

Sir William A. Lane, a world authority on medical matters and long regarded as England's foremost abdominal surgeon, when entertained by the staff of John Hopkins Hospital and Medical College said, "Gentlemen, I will never die of cancer. I am taking measures to prevent it....It is caused by poisons created in our bodies by the food we eat...What we should do, then, if we would avoid cancer, is to eat...raw fruits and vegetables; first, that we may be better nourished; secondly, that we may more easily eliminate waste products...We have been studying germs when we should have been studying diet and drainage...The world has been on the wrong track. The answer has been within ourselves all the time...Drain the body of its poisons, feed it properly, and the miracle is done. Nobody need have cancer who will take the trouble to avoid it." Thank you, Dr. Lane!!!

CHAPTER FIVE — IN REVIEW

1. We live in a drug oriented society...even our water and food are drugged!

2. We take drugs to cure the physical problems often brought on by the taking in of devitalized, processed, and drugged substances into our bodies.

3. A drug, says Webster's Dictionary, is a "substance other than food intended to affect the structure or function of the body."

4. The Bible warns us against the use of all drugs and the deception of drugs!

5. All drugs are poisons to our body!

6. We cannot be drugged or poisoned into health!

7. Health comes only when the body is provided with the proper materials to cleanse the poisons from the systems and rebuild new, living, strong, vital, vibrant cells!!!

8. God made a body that is self-healing and will heal itself when given the opportunity!

6

OTHER DRUGS

".....for by sorceries (drugs) were all nations deceived."
(Revelation 18:23)

In this chapter we will continue our review of drugs as a cause of sickness. Only these drugs are all legal, readily available without prescription, and most of them are consumed by Christians on a regular basis.

As we start our examination of these legal, non-medical drugs, let's remember that a drug is..."A substance other than food intended to affect the structure or function of the body." (Webster's Dictionary)

All of the drugs in this chapter are non-food substances, although most readers of this book will not recognize some of them as drugs. Nor are these drugs normally taken with the intention of affecting the function or structure of the body. None the less, by intent or not, or with knowledge or not, they **all** affect the structure and/or function of the body!!!

We will begin with those that most Christians will readily recognize as drugs and then talk about some drugs that may surprise the average reader...because they are not often recognized as drugs by most Christians!

ALCOHOL

"Wine is a mocker, strong drink is raging: and whosoever is deceived thereby is not wise." (Proverbs 20:1) *"At the last it biteth like a serpent, and stingeth like an adder."* (Proverbs 23:32)

Most Christians recognize alcohol as a drug that destroys, maims and kills! Just on the highways of our nation, some 25,000 people are killed by alcohol each year, while tens of thousands are maimed for the rest of their lives. Then there are the multitudes of broken homes and divorces, along with the abused spouses and children!

Yet, this addictive narcotic drug is a "legal beverage" in most cities and towns in our great nation. There is abundant documentation of alcohol's destructive effect on society! But let's delve into another aspect of beverage alcohol and see **what it does to the body** of the person who consumes it.

ALCOHOL, A DEADLY POISONOUS DRUG

In the process of making beverage alcohol, they begin with a natural, non-drug liquid. If taken into the body in its natural state, this liquid would have a beneficial reaction on the cells of the body (example: grape juice). However, in changing it from a natural state into alcohol, it has to go through a process called fermentation...a process of bacterial action which causes the natural liquid to break down and decay.

The end product of fermentation is alcohol!!! It can be purchased as beer, wine or liquor. What most people do not realize, however, is that alcohol, no matter what form it is in or what it is called, or how legal it may be to purchase, is a deadly poisoning drug!!!

HOW ALCOHOL AFFECTS THE BODY

When alcohol is taken into the body it not only temporarily affects the functioning of the brain, causing people to do all kinds of crazy things under its influence, but it does irreparable damage to the cells, membranes, and tissues as it travels through the body. In fact, it literally destroys body cells while raising havoc with the liver.

If a person continues to use alcohol over a period of time, the liver cells start to die in increasing numbers and these living cells are replaced with scar tissue. As the use of alcohol continues, the liver enlarges and then in the advanced stages of its demise, the liver starts to shrivel and is unable to function. Once the liver reaches this state, an irreversible point has been reached, and death is not far off!

So we see that consuming alcohol is not only un-biblical...a narcotic drug which causes people to do crazy things....a killer on the highways....and a leading cause of broken homes, abuse and divorce.... but the user of this drug is slowly committing suicide, as the alcohol literally destroys the cells of his body!!!

TOBACCO

Many religious groups and churches teach and preach against the use of tobacco...Yet, it is a known fact that many Christians use tobacco!!! For abundant proof of this, stand outside the front door or check the parking lot of almost any church following a church service and see just how many parishioners can't wait to "light up!" Why the rush and urgency to "light up?" ....These people are addicted to the narcotic drug called "nicotine." They are literally "drug addicts," and their body is sceaming for a "fix!"

THE SMOKING SLIPPER

Some Christians try to hide their use of tobacco. I will never forget an incident while I was pastoring a country church some years ago.

In this church there was a deacon that I had in-herited when I became pastor. He smoked cigars, but was always careful not to smoke while I was around.... though his clothes reeked from the cigar smoke.... always a dead give-away!

One day I heard that he was at home sick, so I went to visit him. After knocking on the door, a voice inside said "come in." Obviously he did not realize it was the preacher, because as I entered the room, there was a big cigar in his hand. When he realized who his visitor was, he quickly threw the cigar into his slipper! As the smoke billowed out of that slipper, I made my visit very short lest his slipper go up in smoke also, and he be further embarrassed!

I have often thought of that incident with a chuckle, but it is also very sad. To see people become slaves to the drug nicotine is bad enough, but when you realize what that drug is doing to their body it becomes a tragedy!!!

HOW NICOTINE AFFECTS THE USER

Nicotine is one of the most lethal poisons Americans take into their bodies on a regular basis. It is just as much a narcotic drug as cocaine, marijuana, heroin, opium or morphine. Tobacco smoke contains over 16 different poisons...tars and oxidation products.

God gave us lungs as a means of taking into our bodies clean, pure, fresh air. From this air, the body receives its primary nutritional need...**oxygen!!!** The lungs take in this oxygen and it is sent throughout the body to nourish the cells.

When a person smokes, the lungs become coated and clogged with tars and other poisons from the smoke.... thus causing a malfunction of the lungs! As a result, the body becomes unable to take in sufficient oxygen to meet its needs, and starvation, malnutrition, and enervation of the body results! At the same time, toxins are accumulating in the body because the lungs cannot properly expel them!

Did you ever notice how smokers do not have the wind or stamina to exert themselves physically for any length of time? This is because the lungs cannot take in sufficient oxygen to supply the body's needs!

As the smoker continues this destructive habit, the effects start to manifest themselves in more serious ways. Shortness of breath is often followed by "smokers hack," this is often followed by emphysema, or as I have heard some call it "an asthma attack." Large numbers of smokers ultimately end up with lung cancer or some other form of cancer, circulation problems, heart trouble and an early, horrible, often choking death!!! Every 17 seconds there is a smoking related death!!!

HOW SMOKING AFFECTS OTHERS

If smokers were the only ones harmed by the smoke from cigarette, cigar or pipe, it would be tragic enough....but when others are forced to breathe their smoke it is a double tragedy!!! Smoking in public places where others are forced to breathe second-hand smoke is a crime against humanity!!!

And pity the poor child with a smoking parent or a spouse with a smoking partner. There are ample statistics to show that second-hand smoke is just as harmful to the body of the non-smoker as it is to the smoker himself! Also, statistics show a tremendous increase in respiratory problems of children brought up in a smoker's home!

Most drug addictions result in the destruction of only the addict, while smoking not only harms the addict, but his family, friends, and even total strangers!

A FEW WORDS FOR
SMOKING CHRISTIANS

If you are reading this book and are a smoking Christian, why not quit??? For the sake of yourself, your family, and the Lord who says, *"What? Know ye not that your body is the temple of the Holy Ghost which is in you, which you have of God, and ye are not your own? For ye are bought with a price: Therefore Glorify God in your body, and in your spirit which are God's."* (I Corinthians 6:19-20) Can you in all honesty say, "Smoking glorifies God???"

COFFEE

If America has a national drink, it would have to be coffee. Americans drink coffee with breakfast and sometimes for breakfast. Then in mid-morning they have their "coffee break." It's coffee with lunch, again in mid-afternoon, with supper, etc. Over 2,000,000,000 (two billion) pounds of coffee are consumed by Americans each year.

Coffee drinking seems so innocent and harmless, and I can almost hear some reader saying, "There isn't something wrong with coffee, is there? Does coffee harm the body? Is coffee a drug?

COFFEE IS INDEED A DRUG

Coffee is not a food!!! There is nothing in coffee that the body can use...nothing that will build new cells. The only effect coffee has on the body is to tear it down and destroy the cells.

Coffee is a drug!!! Coffee contains caffeine, along with harmful oils and other toxic substances.

HOW COFFEE AFFECTS THE BODY

Caffeine is a stimulant!!! It is called a stimulant because it excites the nerve-centers into unusual and injurious activity as the body rallies its forces to expel this poison!!! At first, caffeine gives a sensation of exhilaration.....But its after effects are mental depression, nerve exhaustion, decreased muscular power and damage to the liver and kidneys.

When caffeine first enters the body, the blood pressure increases and the heart beats more forcefully, but as the drug is expelled from the body, the heart beats with less force and the blood pressure falls below normal.

Caffeine causes the kidneys to work overtime in an effort to expel this poison, but as coffee drinking continues, the kidneys are weakened and become less efficient. Degeneration of the kidneys is the end result.

The volatile oils in coffee irritate the lining of the stomach and the intestines, causing frequency of urination. This irritation can lead to ulcers, gastritis, spontaneous abortions, still births, premature births, and a host of other problems.

Because the poisoning effects of caffeine on the body are so slow, most coffee drinkers do not realize that their habit is slowly destroying parts of their body!!!

Remember, coffee is not a food....but a poisonous, addictive drug that can only do great harm to the body while it is incapable of doing it any good!!!

TEA

The drug in tea is called "theine." A check of Webster's Dictionary will reveal that "theine" is just another word for "caffeine."

Tea contains about one-half the amount of caffeine as does coffee, but still has the same poisoning effects on the body!!! It just poisons the consumer a little more slowly and takes a little longer to destroy body parts.

COLAS AND SOFT DRINKS

This may come as a surprise, but all cola drinks and most soft drinks contain caffeine!!! And caffeine is an addictive drug!!!

By putting caffeine in colas and soft drinks, a literal addiction is created...which has made the soft drink industry one of the wealthiest industries in the nation. Many children begin their addiction for this drug through the soda bottle!!!

Webster's Dictionary says that "cola" is a "carbonated soft drink flavored with extract from coca leaves, kola nut, sugar, carmel and acid and armotic substances." A further check of Webster's Dictionary reveals that "cocaine" is a bitter crystalline alkaloid...obtained from coca leaves." Regarding the "kola nut", Webster says, "the bitter caffeine-containing seed of a kola tree used...in beverages." We shall discuss the sugar in colas and soft drinks a little later in this chapter.

Those who drink colas and soft drinks containing caffeine, will subject themselves to the same problems by caffeine as we saw under the heading "coffee."

Soft drinks are especially destructive to children.... often causing them to experience irritability, irregular heart beat, insomnia, and hyper-activity, just to name a few.

CHOCOLATE

It may come as a surpise to the reader that chocolate which is derived from the ground, roasted seeds of the cocoa tree, is an addictive drug!!! Cocoa or chocolate contains the drug "theobromine."

Random House Dictionary defines "theobromine" as: "A poisonous powder, used chiefly as a diuretic, myocardial stimulant...found in cocoa." Webster's Dictionary says that "theobromine" is: "a bitter alkaloid...closely related to caffeine...and has stimulant properties."

Chocolate and cocoa are stimulants because when they are taken into the body, the body immediately mobilizes its forces to rid itself of this poisonous drug as quickly as possible. Pimples are just one of the avenues the body uses to try and rid itself of this poisonous drug! And as Webster said, "Theobromine" is a form of "caffeine" and wreaks all of the havoc in the body we learned about under the "coffee" heading.

Isn't it interesting (and pathetic) how many harmful substances we take into our bodies because sugar has been added by the food industry to trick or fool our taste buds into letting them enter! And talking about sugar.....

SUGAR

Glucose is a naturally occuring sugar found in raw fruits, vegetables and honey!!! Glucose is a complex sugar that is released very slowly into the blood stream. Glucose is the form in which God made sugar, and the form in which our all-wise Creator intended sugar to be consumed by the body!

Glucose is very easily and readily assimilated by the body and is a very basic and necessary food.... providing fuel for the cells of the body!!! Webster's Dictionary says of "Glucose," that it is the "form that occurs widely in nature and is the usual form in which carbohydrate is assimilated by animals."

Sucrose on the other hand, is a product of man!!! Sucrose is a physically and mentally addictive drug!!! Sucrose is a simple sugar that is released very quickly into the blood stream....causing great harm to the body!!!

The refiners use some fourteen steps in processing the natural product (usually sugar cane or sugar beets) in the making of sucrose. During this processing the refiners remove the B-complex, the enzymes, proteins, minerals and vitamins.

The heat used in processing, changes the glucose, a natural sugar ($C_6 H_{12} O_6$), into sucrose, an unnatural sugar ($C_{12} H_{22} O_{11}$)! This processing, produces an unstable chemical substance, containing no vitamins, minerals or food value!!! It is just pure carbohydrate!!! And it is capable of doing tremendous harm to the body!!!

MOST PROCESSED FOOD CONTAIN SUCROSE

A careful reading of the ingredient labels on food products found on the super market shelves, would reveal sugar or salt, or both, in almost every manufactured product. Without sugar and/or salt, the food manufacturers would not be able to sell their products....our taste buds would reject these dead, devitalized, toxic, so-called "food" products!!! You will even find sugar or salt in such products as toothpaste, mouth wash, tobacco, chewing gum, etc.

SUGAR (SUCROSE) IS ADDICTIVE

The average American begins his addiction to sugar shortly after birth when a nurse puts a bottle of sugar water in the infant's mouth. This is followed by adding sugar to the infants formula so the baby will drink this unnatural substance. The commercial baby food industry puts sugar into their processed food products so the babies' taste buds will not reject these unnatural products.

Then there are the breakfast cereals, many of which contain in excess of 50% sugar! Ice cream usually contains about 33% sugar! A twelve-ounce can or bottle of cola or soft drink contains about eight teaspoons of sugar....and that is just the beginning of an endless list!!!

At the turn of the century, the annual consumption of sugar in the form of sucrose was approximately seven pounds for every person in the United States. By 1964, this figure had jumped to around 95 pounds. Today, the average intake of sucrose by every man, woman and child in our country is in excess of 125 pounds!!! We have literally become a nation of sugar addicts!!!

At creation, God placed in man a natural desire for sugar (glucose)!!! However, the commercial food industry has taken this God-given natural desire for natural sugar and used it to make tremendous profit on an unsuspecting public!!! They have substituted sucrose for glucose, and thus fooled and perverted man's taste buds!!!

WHAT AFFECT SUCROSE HAS ON OUR BODIES

Sucrose has a toxic, poisoning, drugging affect on the body!!! When sugar is consumed in the form of sucrose, it ferments in the body, causing the formation of carbonic acid, acetic acid and alcohol.

Acetic acid is very destructive to the cells of the body, literally burning them. It also has a paralyzing effect on the nerves. The alcohol can cause reactions similar in behavior to beverage alcohol.....even to the extent of violent actions!!! The alcohol also has a damaging effect on the kidneys. It affects the nerve and brain functions of the body, especially concentration, observation and locomotion.

As consumption of unnatural sugar continues, the pancreas starts to have problems! The large volume of sucrose causes the pancreas to be tremendously overworked and it begins to malfunction. Many problems can result.....probably two of the most serious are hypoglycemia and diabetes!

Most readers are familiar with diabetes, but hypoglycemia creates unbelievable problems as well..... and the sad thing is that most of those who suffer from it aren't aware they even have it. Some of the symptoms of hypoglycemia are headaches, irritability, depression, fatigue, inability to concentrate, being upset with spouse or children for no apparent reason, etc. Some marriage counselors familiar with hypoglycemia estimate that upwards of 50% of all marriage problems can be traced to this condition!

Sucrose also leaches vitamin "B" from the body, destroys calcium, shatters the nervous system, causes teeth to decay, hair to fall out, senility, circulation problems, heart trouble, and a host of others.

Just drinking one 12 oz. can or bottle of coke or soda a day will add 12 pounds of weight to the body in a year...because of its high sugar (sucrose) content! Many studies have shown sucrose to be one of the main causes of discipline problems with children, and often the root cause leading to alcoholism, crime, rape, murder and a host of other social ills!!!

Most Christians consume large amounts of sucrose daily!!! You might find it interesting to check your daily intake! Read the ingredient label of every processed food item that you purchase...the closer the word "sugar" is to the beginning of the listing, the higher the percentage of sugar in that product!

Dr. C. Samuel West, in his book "The Golden Seven Plus One" states on page 102...."If you fail to do something about your 'simple' sugar intake, beginning today, you will be committing willful suicide!"

SALT

Salt in the form of sodium chloride is a deadly, poisonous, addicting drug and possibly the greatest killer of mankind!!!

For years, the medical profession told us that it was necessary to take additional salt or salt tablets into our body during hot weather when the body was sweating excessively. They reasoned: "The large amounts of salt being excreted from the pores of the body had to be replaced!" After causing untold physical suffering for mankind, due to their lack of understanding of how the human body functions, they finally acknowledged that they were wrong. Now the medical profession has reversed itself and says we should not take extra salt into our bodies, but rather eliminate salt from our diet or at least cut down drastically on our consumption.

Earth salt, or even sea salt, is an inorganic form of sodium which cannot be utilized by the body!!! It enters the body as sodium chloride and what the body can't eliminate through the urine or sweat glands is stored in the tissues of the body as sodium chloride! When it is finally able to exit from the body, it is still sodium chloride! But it has left a trail of woe and destruction all along the way, from entry to exit!!!

What was really happening when the medical profession found all of that sodium chloride exiting the body through the sweat glands.....was that the body was using the pores as a means of ridding itself of this deadly poison!!! God has made such a marvelous body....always trying to cleanse the temple of toxic substance and keep itself clean and pure!!!

HOW SALT AFFECTS THE BODY

When SALT, in the form of sodium chloride, enters the body it draws water from the blood stream, causing the body to send out an SOS signal that manifests itself in thirst! An example would be: After consuming a bowl of soup, which usually contains lots of salt, the body sends a signal to the brain: "Help! Send water!" Why??? Because the water helps dilute the salt concentration in order to help neutralize its poisoning of the body!

However, most people consume so much salt (salt is found in almost every commercial food product), that the body can't get all the salt out of the system, so it is carried by the blood and deposited throughout the body in the tissue fluids in an effort to dilute its devastating effects. When a person goes on a fast, he can lose as much as 10 pounds or more in just a few days from the excessive body fluids retained in an effort to neutralize the salt.

These salt deposits are found throughout the body and cause unbelievable harm. Some physical problems caused by salt are....hardening of the arteries, arthritis, ulcers, distorted vision and even blindness, high blood pressure, tumors, cancer, and a multitude of other degenerative disorders.

Salt is an antibiotic; it kills life!!! It is used as a preservative because it kills the bacteria (life) in the food to prevent the natural decomposing of that food. In the body, it is just as much a destroyer and killer of cells and life itself!

Salt begins its addictive influence in the life of a little child when mother, after cooking all of the flavor and nutrition out of the food, adds salt in an effort to make it taste good according to her taste buds. Most purchased baby foods are also cooked, often with added salt. When this salted, cooked food is first placed into the baby's mouth.....it is usually spit back out. So what does the person feeding the baby do?.....Push it back in! Baby spits it back out again.....and the parent forces it back into the young childs mouth until it is accepted.....and thus the addiction to salt begins!! Granted, it was done in ignorance, but how sad!!

Does the body have a need for sodium? Yes, but only in trace amounts, and that sodium must be in an organic form for the body to be able to utilize it. Organic sodium occurs naturally in most all raw fruits and vegetables!!!

GOD GAVE US A MARVELOUS BODY

As we learn of all the terrible harmful substances we have been putting into our body for so many years, the first reaction one often has is, "It's a miracle we are still alive."

The reason we are still alive, however, is because our wonderful Creator made such a marvelous body that it will take abuse after abuse, always making every effort to cleanse and rebuild itself until it can just take no more abuse. At this point it starts to manifest the years of abuse and neglect, with the weakest part of the body breaking down first. If the diet and life-style is not changed at this point, and the abuse halted, the breakdown will continue to the next weakest part of the body, etc.

The bodies of some individuals can withstand more abuse than others.....possibly because of extensive exercise, which helps flush out toxins, or possibly because of inheriting physically strong ancestral stock. But you can count on all abusers having a payday some day, because of an irreversible law which says: *"Be not deceived; God is not mocked: for whatsoever a man soweth (in ignorance or with knowledge), that shall he also reap."* (Galatians 6:7)

Fortunately, even after the body starts to break down, the body will usually respond and rebuild the damaged cells when we cooperate with it, stop abusing, start cleansing, and then properly feed our body....."God's temple!!!"

"Why Christians Get Sick" and are just as sick

as non-Christians and why spiritual Christians are just as sick as Christians that are not as spiritual, should already be evident to every reader of this book.....our diet and life-styles have been the same!!!

CHAPTER SIX — IN REVIEW

1. Just because a drug is "legal" and readily available does not make it good for the body!
2. All drugs affect the structure and function of the body!
3. The consuming of alcohol is not only unbiblical, a narcotic drug causing people to do crazy things, a destroyer of lives on the highway and a leading cause of divorce, but also the committing of slow suicide, as it literally destroys the cells of the body, which is the temple of God!
4. Tobacco, a narcotic drug, contains some 16 different poisons which coat the lungs and keep them from functioning properly and slowly kills the user and those around him!
5. Coffee contains the drug, caffeine, which can cause a multitude of physical problems!
6. Tea, cola, soft drinks and chocolate all contain the drug caffeine and all are extremely harmful to the body!
7. Sugar, in the form of "sucrose" is a drug that is very addictive and creates many of our physical and emotional and even social problems!
8. Salt is a deadly poisonous drug and possibly the greatest killer of mankind!
9. Fortunately, even after the body starts to break down, the body will usually respond and rebuild the damaged cells when we cooperate with it, stop abusing, start cleansing, and then properly feed our body....."God's temple!!!"

7

INSUFFICIENT EXERCISE

"In the sweat of thy face shalt thou eat bread..."
(Genesis 3:19)

When God created man, He made him to be physically active!!! How do we know this to be true?

FIRST, BECAUSE GOD **COMMANDS** IT!

"And the Lord God took the man, and put him into the Garden of Eden to dress it ('cultivate it' Webster) *and to keep it* ('take charge of as a caretaker' Webster)*."* (Genesis 2:15)

"Therefore the Lord God sent him forth from the Garden of Eden, to till (to work by plowing, sowing, and raising crops' Webster) *the ground from whence he was taken."* (Genesis 3:23)

"Six days shalt thou labour, and do thy work:" (Exodus 20:9)

"If any man would not work neither should he eat. For we hear that there are some which walk among you disorderly, working not at all, but are busybodies. Now them that are such we command and exhort by our Lord Jesus Christ that with quietness they work, and eat their own bread ('food' Webster)*."* (II Thessalonians 3:10)

SECONDLY, BY **EXAMPLE!**

"And Noah began to be an husbandman ('one that plows and cultivates land: farmer).*"* (Genesis 9:20)

75

THIRDLY, THE BODY **CANNOT FUNCTION PROPERLY WITHOUT IT!**

When we study the body and how it was made to function, we learn that the body cannot function properly without daily, vigorous, physical movement!!!

GOD CREATED MAN TO BE PHYSICALLY ACTIVE

When God made man, he placed him in *a garden* — Genesis 2:15. In this garden, God provided the food man was to eat — (Genesis 1:29; 2:9, 16). However, after the fall, there were "thorns and thistles" (Genesis 3:18), what we would call weeds, that hindered the growing of man's food. So in order to grow the food man needed to sustain life, it was necessary for him to remove the weeds. This required physical exertion!!!

From the time of creation, until quite recently, man physically labored for his food on almost a daily basis! Why, it was just a few hundred years ago that our founding fathers came to the shores of this great land and carved out clearings, made gardens, and thus physically labored for their food. Thanksgiving was the celebration of an abundant harvest.

THE IMPORTANCE OF GARDENING

All through history, the major pursuit of man has been the growing of his own food!!! In fact, the growing of one's own food supply was practiced by the majority of people until not too many years ago. One of the great tragedies of recent generations has been the leaving of the land by multitudes of people!

If you are 50 years of age or older, it is probable that your parents or at least your grandparents were farmers! I can still see my grandmother in her 80's out in the garden before the sun was up, hoeing the weeds between the rows of vegetables. I can remember my grandfather guiding a plow that was being pulled by his horse as he broke up the ground for the garden.

They outlived their daughter, my mother, by almost

a quarter of a century. My Mom (a country girl) married my Dad (a city boy) and moved to the city, bought her food, and lived a very physically inactive life.

What I am trying to say, is that God made man to be physically active on a daily basis!!! This physical activity was to be performed in the great out-of-doors in the fresh air!

LEAVING THE LAND HAS HAD ITS PRICE

As man has gotten away from the way God intended him to live, man's physical body has paid a terrible price! In fact, I dare say that the average American at age 40 couldn't physically keep up with my farmer grandparents when they were 80!

Americans of today, may like being able to open a can of food or take a package of frozen food from the freezer, or open a box or package or even go to the super market and buy fresh (?) produce, but the physical toll they are paying for these conveniences is incalculable!!! This easy source of food, without requiring physical labor in exchange, has produced multitudes of physical problems, great physical suffering and early deaths!!!

So we now find ourselves in this present day, not only eating processed, packaged foods almost totally devoid of nutritional value, loaded with chemicals, but no physical exercise was required to obtain them!!!

WHY THE BODY NEEDS PHYSICAL ACTIVITY

In order for the body to sustain physical life, four basic ingredients are necessary!!! These ingredients are:

AIR (OXYGEN)
WATER
FOOD
EXERCISE

Food is the LEAST important of these basic needs, as you can usually live well in excess of 40 days without food. Without water you can't live more than 4 days and without air you can't live more than 4 minutes. However, without motion, the body cells will slowly die!!!

The reason the body needs physical activity is that the tissue cells of which the body is composed require daily stimulating to maintain their elasticity and pliability. If they are not exercised on a regular basis, they will become weak, sickly, and begin to malfunction. Ultimately, if these cells continue to go without exercise, they will cease to function and rather than reproducing healthy, vital, vibrant new cells as God designed them to do, these cells slowly die, and their deposits accumulate and add to the accumulation of toxins and debris in the body.

THE LYMPH

The soft tissue cells of the body are constantly bathed in a watery fluid called lymph. This lymph has several vitally important functions, which are basically.....feeding and cleansing the cells! But unlike the blood, which has a pump (the heart) to move the blood through the body, the lymph has no pump!

Because it has no pump, the lymph must depend on the motion or exercise of the body! When the body is exercised vigorously on a regular basis, the lymph moves and performs its feeding and cleansing functions as God intended. But when the body is not exercised, the feeding and cleansing of the body by the lymph is hampered, and the toxins and debris begin to accumulate throughout the body. Deposits of debris further restrict the cleansing of the lymph.

As deposits continue to accumulate, the body cells are cut off from their supply of fresh air (oxygen) and are unable to remove the debris (carbon dioxide and other wastes). Also, the cells are prevented from receiving new building supplies. The whole system begins to malfunction, resulting in a multitude of physical problems, including cancer and ultimately death!

TONSILS AND APPENDIX

It is interesting to note that swollen tonsils are one of God's warning devices! When the lymph is burdened with too heavy a load of poisons in the system, the tonsils swell. The medical profession says, "give the sufferer a drug," which will short circuit the warning signal. If the drugs do not work, "cut them out." The doctor removed mine when I was a small child!

Interestingly, all four of our children had bad tonsil problems and the doctor gave them drugs for this condition for years.....finally the doctor wanted to remove them from all four. It was at about this time we learned about diet and health....So rather than having them cut out, we changed their diet and all of the tonsil problems ceased!!!

The appendix has a function similar to the tonsils..... they also swell when the lymph system is overburdened with toxic waste. The medical profession treats the appendix in a similar manner as they do tonsils.....if there is a problem, "cut them out!" When God created man, He didn't make any spare or useless parts!!!

MUSCLES

Without exercise, the muscles begin to atrophy ('decrease in size or wasting away' Webster). This is clearly evident when you start to use muscles that have not been exercised in a while. But the most important muscle affected by lack of exercise is the heart muscle!!!

Without exercise, the heart starts to malfunction, arteries clog, strokes and heart attacks result. Many deaths occur every year when people suddenly put a heavy exertion on an unexercised heart. Shoveling snow would be a good example of this.

THE IMPORTANCE OF EXERCISE

In my sixteen years of studying the body and how nutrition and exercise relate to it, I have found that a person who exercises vigorously on a regular basis and yet eats a poor diet will usually experience less physical problems than the person who eats well but does not exercise! The obvious reason.....The person who exercises is better able to remove the toxins and debris from the system!

Without daily, vigorous exercise, tissue cells lose their elasticity, lymph cannot move adequately to cleanse and feed body cells, muscles atrophy, the body does not receive a sufficient supply of oxygen, arteries clog, mental faculties are slowed, people become forgetful and eventually senile, and death finally results!!!

There are many other problems caused by insufficient exercise, but hopefully we have shown enough to convince the reader that insufficient, daily, vigorous exercise is one of the leading causes as to **"Why Christians Get Sick!!!"**

CHAPTER SEVEN — IN REVIEW

1. God made man to be physically active!
2. Man's primary physical activity was to be received through the labor necessary to grow his own food supply!
3. Until recent years, most people raised their own food supply!
4. Convenience foods and the easy availability of food for purchase has dramatically reduced the amount of exercise the average man receives and has produced correspondingly increased physical problems!
5. To sustain life, four basic ingredients are necessary.....(1) AIR (oxygen), (2) WATER, (3) FOOD, (4) MOTION OR EXERCISE!
6. Without daily, vigorous exercise, tissue cells lose their elasticity!
7. Without daily, vigorous exercise, lymph cannot move adequately to cleanse and feed body cells!

8. Without daily, vigorous exercise, muscles atrophy ('decrease in size or wasting away' Webster)!

9. Without daily, vigorous exercise, the body does not receive a sufficient supply of oxygen, arteries clog, mental faculties are slowed, people become forgetful and eventually senile, and death finally results!

10. Insufficient vigorous daily exercise is one of the leading causes of **"Why Christians Get Sick?"**

8

STRESS AND NEGATIVE EMOTIONS

"And the peace of God, which passeth all understanding, shall keep your hearts and minds through Christ Jesus. Finally, brethren, whatsoever things are true, whatsoever things are honest, whatsoever things are just, whatsoever things are pure, whatsoever things are lovely, whatsoever things are of good report; if there be any virtue, and if there be any praise, think on these things.....for I have learned, in whatsoever state I am, therewith to be content."

(Philippians 4:7-8, 11)

During my nearly twenty years in the ministry, coming in contact with multitudes of Christians, I found an usually high percentage of Christians with emotional problems. In fact, there are many ministries that deal exclusively with Christians who have emotional problems.

Now emotional problems are definitely a form of sickness; however, it is a sickness that many do not want to recognize or acknowledge as a sickness. In fact, many do not want to acknowledge that they even have a problem. And sadly, when help is finally sought, the help often does not deal with the cause, but rather with the symptoms.

JESUS WANTS US TO BE HAPPY

As we read the Bible, we have to come to the conclusion that the Lord wants us to be happy!!! *"Blessed is everyone that feareth the Lord; that walketh in his ways....happy shalt thou be, and it shall be well with thee."* (Psalm 128:1-2) *"Happy is that people whose God is the Lord."* (Psalm 144:15) *"....and whoso trusteth in the Lord, happy is he."* (Proverbs 16:20) Jesus said: *".....I am come that they might have life, and that they might have it more abundantly."* (John 10:10)

ARE CHRISTIANS HAPPY?

But how many Christians do you personally know who are living a really happy, abundant, vibrant Christian life??? And if not, why not???

It seems that in many Christian circles, there is a tendency to blame everything on sin! If you are sick, someone will invariably say, "You need to get your heart right with the Lord." Or if unhappy, they might say, "You know, if you were right with the Lord, you would be happy!"

Thus, we are led to believe that all physical and emotional problems have a spiritual cause. It's interesting how we tend to blame God for what we don't understand, or base all of our problems on a spiritual cause.

Now I am not saying that sin can't be "A" cause, but I believe the cause is usually something more tangible. And there are other causes for emotional problems!!!

TWO KINDS OF EMOTIONS

There are only two kinds of emotions!!! All emotions are either (1) positive or (2) negative!!! If we were somehow able to keep track of a person's emotions and put each emotion into a positive or negative column, the negative column would be the big winner with the majority of Christians! How tragic!!!

Emotions are simply "feelings" which are stimulated by the mental and/or physical parts of our body. However, these emotions are so powerful that they affect our lives and those around us probably more than anyone realizes.

POSITIVE EMOTIONS

When we feel joy or love or happiness or peace or contentment, which are all positive emotions, there is a radiation of pleasant influences throughout the body and even to those around us. These positive emotions have a positive effect on the functioning of our whole being, even to the promotion of good physical health!

But which comes first, the chicken or the egg? As Christians, the answer to that question is easy.....the chicken, because God created everything whole! In the case of emotions, which comes first....the positive emotion producing a healthy body, or a healthy body producing a healthy, positive mind? In the majority of cases, the overwhelming evidence favors the latter, but not always!

PERSONAL EXPERIENCE

In my own experience, I found that as my body responded physically to my new life style, and I became physically stronger, my emotions became more positive. And I must confess that my thinking had degenerated to a very low state before I changed my life-style.

So I found, personally, that my poor diet and lack of vigorous exercise resulted in negative thinking. When I changed my diet and started daily, vigorous exercise, taking into my lungs copious amounts of oxygen, my body started to heal, and my emotions became increasingly more positive.

In fact, when I do my jogging, I often experience what some would call a mild "high", a state of euphoria and well being. I have also found that during jogging my mental faculties become very keen and I can do some of my clearest thinking and make my best decisions. Nutritional doctors tell us that one of the greatest anti-depresants available is vigorous exercise.

NEGATIVE EMOTIONS

A body that is not functioning properly, whether due to a cold, headache, or more serious physical problem, will tend to lead a person to experience negative emotions.

The problem then compounds itself. These physical problems produce negative emotions. The negative emotions rob valuable energy from the body which hinders the body's efforts to cleanse and heal itself.

Because the body is hindered in its cleansing and healing efforts, the stress produces more negative emotions. This vicious cycle snowballs and the results can be devastating!!! Sadly, there are multitudes of Christians who find themselves in such a predicament.

Feelings of fear, worry, sorrow, hate, jealousy, anger and the like, radiate a negative influence throughout the body. They also radiate negativism to the people around us. These negative emotions short-circuit the normal functioning of the body, thus harmfully affecting the body. Our bodies literally run on electrical current energy, and negative emotions dissipate this energy!

MANY CHRISTIANS HAVE
EMOTIONAL PROBLEMS

Christians have so many emotional problems, yet seldom understand the reason why. And when they are faced with an emotional problem, the tendency is often to blame everybody and everything else for the problem, usually refusing to accept that the problem is within...they are the problem!!!

Some people turn to drugs in an effort to escape from

these negative emotions; yes, even Christians. Some turn to the drugs that come in the form of pills in a little bottle. Some turn to alcohol. For some, temporary emotional relief may be found in tobacco, coffee, sugar, chocolate, or one of the most popular, constant snacking.

All of the drugs we learned about in Chapter Six cause negative thinking and depression!!! If there is any relief, it is only temporary at best, and ultimately these drugs compound the situation!

Sugar is one of the cruelest culprits affecting the emotions, as it causes a malfunction of the organs regulating our blood sugar levels. High sugar intake causes the blood sugar levels to fluctuate excessively, sending people onto an emotional roller coaster. You might like to go back and re-read Chapter Six in this regard.

NEGATIVE INPUT

As to the cause for negative emotions among Christians, there is another side of the coin. On the one side we have physical problems producing negative emotions. On the other side we have negative input producing negative emotions....which produce physical problems!!!

We teach our teens: "You will become what you hang around! What you read, what you listen to, what you see, all goes into your computer/brain and programs it with good or bad, positive or negative. What goes in is what will come out! Garbage in....garbage out!!!

The Bible says, *"Be not deceived; God is not mocked: for whatsoever a man soweth, that shall he also reap."* (Galatians 6:7) This is an irreversible law!!!

SOAP OPERAS

For example, it is exceedingly difficult for people to maintain a positive and healthy outlook concerning romance and marriage when they feed their minds on the TV "soaps" In these "soaps" husbands and wives cheat on their spouses, there is physical abuse, alcohol, divorce, and all kinds of sordid happenings.

What is the result of this negative input in the lives of the viewers? Multitudes of marriages have been affected adversely, even resulting in divorces.

Most of the television programming of today is negative! Many Christians feed on programs that feature violence, murder, rape, war, abuse, lawbreaking, drugs, stealing, etc., etc. The average preschooler watches 30 hours of TV a week. By age 16, that child will have watched 16,000 hours of TV compared to only 12,000 hours in school! This amount of negative input can do incalculable harm!

The words of many of the songs of today promote the negative, including drugs, alcohol and unfaithfulness! Even the news casts seem always to feature the negative events of the world!

WHAT CAN CHRISTIANS DO?

Any Christian who wants to live a happy, abundant, Christian life, must SHUN as many negative inputs as possible!!! Why? Because these negative inputs produce negative thinking.....which produces an unhappy person and disastrously affects his life, his future, and all with whom he comes in contact!!!

These negative thoughts and feelings also have a negative effect on the body and short-circuits its operation. Negative emotions, stress and depression can create many physical problems!!!

EXCESSIVE NEGATIVE INPUT IN THE CHURCH

Before concluding this chapter, I would like to touch on an area that has become an increasing concern to me the longer I am involved in the Lord's work.....and that is, excessive negative input in our churches!!! And remember....this is coming from a preacher!!!

When I was in school preparing for the ministry, we had a guest speaker who spoke to us "preacher boys." The main thrust of his message was: "If you want to be a great preacher and build a big church, you must preach against things! It doesn't matter what it is, just preach against it!"

This particular message left a very deep impression on me; so much so, that it became the major approach in my preaching for many, many years. But as time went by, I was less and less pleased with the product this type of approach was producing in the people to whom I ministered.

Now certainly, as Christians, we must be against things — Jesus was!!! But we must not be so obsessed with the negative that we relegate the positive to a secondary position or eliminate it altogether! We must not be guilty of encouraging negative thinking!

THE GOSPEL — A POSITIVE MESSAGE

THE GOSPEL MESSAGE IS.....**A POSTIVE MESSAGE!!!!!**

I. **GOD LOVES US!** (John 3:16)
II. **JESUS PAID MAN'S SIN DEBT** ON THE OLD RUGGED CROSS! (I Peter 2:24) JESUS DIED, WAS BURIED **BUT ROSE AGAIN!** (I Corinthians 15:3-4)
III. **JESUS FORGIVES AND SAVES SIN-NERS** WHEN THEY BELIEVE THE GOSPEL MESSAGE AND PERSONALLY ASK JESUS INTO THEIR HEART TO BE THEIR SAV-IOUR! (John 1:12; Colossians 2:13)
IV. **THE HOLY SPIRIT COMES TO DWELL WITHIN EACH BELIEVER....**GUIDING HIM IN HIS DAILY LIFE! (I Corinthians 3:16; John 16:13)
V. **HEAVEN IS ASSURED** THE CHRISTIAN AT THE END OF THIS LIFE! (II Corinthians 5:8)

VI. **JESUS IS COMING AGAIN** TO TAKE CHRISTIANS TO THEIR HEAVENLY HOME!
"For the Lord himself shall descend from heaven with a shout, with the voice of the archangel, and with the trump of God: and the dead in Christ shall rise first: then we which are alive and remain shall be caught up together with them in the clouds, to meet the Lord in the air: and so shall we ever be with the Lord. Wherefore comfort one another with these words." I Thessalonians 4:16-18)

THAT IS A **POSITIVE** MESSAGE FROM BEGINNING TO END!!!!! CHRISTIANS OUGHT TO BE THE **HAPPIEST** PEOPLE ON EARTH!!!!!
CHRISTIANS **PERSONALLY KNOW THE CREATOR!**
THEY **KNOW** WHERE THEY CAME FROM!
THEY **KNOW** WHY THEY ARE HERE!
THEY **KNOW** WHERE THEY ARE GOING WHEN THIS LIFE IS OVER!!!!!

NEEDED, A POSITIVE CHRISTIANITY

How desperately we need a positive approach to Christianity, from every pastor, church worker, and Christian! Too often it seems that Christians have a gloom and doom complex, and it has produced many emotional and physical problems. My brethren, these things ought not so to be!

Many people in the world have shunned Christianity because they think it is only a religion of don'ts and many of the Christians they come in contact with are anything but positive and happy.

The world needs to see a consistent, positive Christianity!!! Christians need to accentuate the positive for their own mental and physical well-being as well as to show a negative old world something different! Something better!!!

Christians ought to be the healthiest and happiest people on the face of this earth!!!

CHAPTER EIGHT — IN REVIEW

1. Many Christians experience emotional problems!
2. There are only two kinds of emotions — positive and negative!
3. Positive emotions contribute to happiness and health!
4. Negative emotions produce unhappiness and physical problems!
5. Physical problems contribute greatly to negative emotions!
6. Drugs cause rather than relieve negative emotions!
7. Improving one's physical health through diet and vigorous exercise will lead to more positive emotions!
8. Negative input can also produce negative emotions!
9. We become what we program into our computer/brain! *"For whatsoever a man soweth, that shall he also reap."*
10. The Gospel message is a positive message!
11. The world needs to see a positive Christianity!
12. Christians ought to be the healthiest and happiest people on the face of the earth!!!

9

THE VIOLATIONS OF GOD'S NATURAL LAWS

"For by him were all things created, that are in heaven, and that are in earth, visible and invisible....all things were created by him...and by him all things consist (are held together)." (Colossians 1:16-17) *"And God saw everything that he had made, and, behold, it was very good."* Genesis 1:31)

From the above verses we see that at creation, God not only made a perfect creation, but also established natural laws to perpetuate this perfection! These were natural laws by which His creation would be governed.

Without these natural laws, His creation would not be able to sustain itself!

NATURAL LAWS

An example of God's natural laws would be the law of gravity, a law that we are all very familiar with. This law was established at creation for the purpose of maintaining order and to allow man to move about the earth with safety. If God had not established this law, life on earth would be chaotic at best!

It is interesting to note that though this law was established at creation, man was not aware of the existance of this law of gravity until comparatively recent years. Did the lack of knowledge of this law's existence nullify the consequences of breaking it??? Of course not!!!

Regardless of whether man knows of a law's existence or not, violations of that law bring a penalty to the violator. An example would be when a person gets too close to the edge of a high cliff and somehow falls off. This person may land on the rocks below and be killed! Why? Because he violated a natural law!!!

Likewise, the person who touches a hot stove will get burned! Someone steps in front of a moving vehicle will be injured or killed! A person who for some reason, keeps his head under water for a comparatively short period of time will drown! These burns, injuries and deaths would all be the result of breaking a natural law!!!

NATURAL LAWS ARE IMPERSONAL

All of the above occurrences are the result of the violation of natural laws, and the laws that caused them are totally impersonal!!! Violation of natural laws will result in sickness, injury, or untimely death whether the violator realized the law existed or not; whether the violator was a Christian or not; whether the violator was a spiritual Christian or not! The law will automatically be applied whether a man knows of the existence of the law or not!!! Ignorance of a law makes absolutely no difference in the consequences of breaking it!!!

THE NATURAL LAWS OF HEALTH AND HEALING

God created man to be well and to have perfect health!!! God programmed man's brain to respond automatically to foreign matter entering the body, or to injury to the body. This has been programmed into every person from Adam and Eve's children right down to you and me through the DNA (the molecular basis of heredity which contains the master plans for building the body), and the RNA (cellular chemical activities which enables the body to follow these plans).

When a person sustains a cut, the victim may cleanse the area or a doctor may put in some stitches to close the wound, but it is the brain that automatically sets in motion the healing process!!! Then, we can see the miracle of healing take place right before our very eyes!

Most of us have personally experienced this healing in our own bodies and we can recall cuts, bumps, bruises and burns we have had in the past, that have healed!

SICKNESS IS NOT NATURAL

The fact that God programmed healing into our brain is proof that God does not want man to be sick!!!

When a person becomes sick, it is because a natural law has been violated! Period!!! There are no other reasons!!! (Excepting those we talked about in Chapter 3, when the sickness was for God's glory or because of sin.)

If a sick person wants to get well, that person must stop violating the law that caused the sickness in the first place and start cooperating with that law!!! It is all so very simple when one understands God's laws!

It is also very important to understand that sickness is the body's effort to heal itself, and that sickness is just the manifestation of this healing effort!!! An example of this would be what we call the "common cold" that we talked about in an earlier chapter.

Other efforts of the body to cleanse and heal itself are manifested in fevers, swollen glands, tonsilitis, appendicitis, pimples, etc. When these manifestations are ignored or drugged or surgically removed in order to suppress the symptoms, the results will usually lead to a more serious sickness or even an untimely death!

PERSONAL ACCOUNTABILITY

Many people have a problem accepting personal responsibility for their own health problems. It is a lot easier to believe that some germ or virus or outside influence over which they had no control caused their physical problem, than it is to acknowledge that they personally caused the problem themselves! Often, because of ignorance, people will even blame God or say that it is "God's will", thus, once again, shifting the blame away from themselves.

The Bible continually teaches personal accountability! *"Be not deceived; God is not mocked: for whatsoever a man soweth, that shall he also reap."* (Galatians 6-7) And again: *"Know ye not that ye* (your body is) *the temple of God, and that the spirit of God dwelleth in you? If any man defile* ('corrupts the purity or perfection of' (Webster) *the temple of God, him shall God destroy* ('put out of existence' (Webster) *for the temple of God is holy, which temple ye are."* (I Corinthians 3:16-17) Read that scripture again!!!

Health laws are simply irreversible natural laws established by God!!! In this regard it matters not if you are a Christian or a non-Christian, spiritual or unspiritual.... *"For he (God) maketh his sun to rise on the evil and on the good and sendeth rain on the just and on the unjust."* (Matthew 5:45)

If a person violates God's natural laws pertaining to the body and health, that person will personally reap the consequences of that violation sooner or later! It is inevitable!!!

THE BODY CAN TAKE GREAT ABUSE

In Chapter Two we learned a little about the marvelous body God made for man. In Chapters four through eight, we saw some of the things man does to his body that causes him to have physical problems.

If the body reacted immediately and violently when we put something into it that was not natural or for our well being, perhaps that would help. But often people ignore even the body's violent protests and reactions!!!

No doubt there are people reading this book who can remember the violent reaction of the body the first time they inhaled cigarette smoke, yet they continued to inhale that vile, toxic smoke!

After ignoring the reaction of the body's warning devices over a period of time, the warning devices became paralyzed or deadened, until there was no more protest from the body. Now, the smoker could puff, puff, puff his life away a little more with each cigarette without the body even offering any resistence. Not realizing that they were violating a natural law...A law that declares "Man's lungs require pure air!!!"

HOW THE BODY MANIFESTS
THESE VIOLATIONS

Colds, fevers, headaches, stomach aches, indigestion, heart burn, tonsillitis, appendicitis, pimples, boils, rashes, body odor, arthritis, asthma, kidney stones, gall stones, cirrhosis, constipation, diabetes, heart failure, stroke, high blood pressure, obesity, pneumonia, tumors, varicose veins, cancer, etc., etc., etc. are all manifestations by the body of violations of God's natural laws!!!

God made a marvelous body, and that is the reason it continues to function even after abuse is heaped upon abuse while the body continually makes the effort to cleanse, repair and rebuild itself.

This cleansing and rebuilding process was built into man's brain when he was created, and it has been passed along to every person born into this world from Adam and Eve to you and me.

However, no matter how marvelous a body God made, there is a point where the body cannot contend with or tolerate any more abuse, and it starts to break down at its weakest point, usually the area that has received the greatest abuse or possibly where there has been an inherited weakness!

CIGARETTES, ALCOHOL, COFFEE, ETC.

For the cigarette smoker it is usually the lungs that break down first, although all of the body suffers from the use of tobacco. Sadly, this breakdown does not usually manifest itself until serious harm has already taken place in the body.

The person who consumes alcohol or coffee or tea or soft drinks will generally find the liver being the organ that starts to fail first.

The cocaine and marijuana user will find the brain cells are being destroyed and those who smoke marijuana will also suffer similar problems to that of the cigarette smoker. In fact, marijuana smoke contains FOUR TIMES the tars and carbon monoxide as does cigarette smoke.

The sugar user will find the pancreas and related organs malfunctioning, resulting in blood sugar problems, as we talked about in Chapter Eight.

All abuses or violations have a negative and destructive effect on the body!!! What are called "sickness" and "disease" are manifestions of the body's efforts to cleanse and heal itself!!! If the abuse does not stop at this point, the problem compounds and ultimately results in an early and untimely and "unexpected" death!!!

THE BODY IS SELF HEALING

Earlier in this chapter we learned that there are natural laws for health and healing. We saw this natural law of healing in action when a cut, bruise or burn healed itself right before our very eyes.

Most Christians, as well as non-Christians, have violated many of the natural laws of health! I know that I was personally in violation of many of them for a good part of my life. As a result of my own violations I had some very serious physical problems.

In the next chapter, we want to examine God's natural laws of health and healing. We will learn what these laws are. We will learn that, when observed, these laws will not only keep well those who apply them, but will bring healing to most of the physical problems that already exist!!!

CHAPTER NINE — IN REVIEW

1. When God made man, He established natural laws to govern His creation!
2. God's creation was perfect and His natural laws were designed to perpetuate that perfection!
3. Natural laws are impersonal! They apply equally to everyone.....Christian or non-Christian!
4. Sickness and disease are not natural but are the body's effort to cleanse and heal itself after natural laws have been violated!
5. Each person is personally accountable for his or her own health! Man cannot blame someone or something else for his own physical breakdowns!
6. The body can take a tremendous amount of abuse but there is a limit, and all abuses will eventually manifest themselves in physical problems!

10

GOD'S NATURAL LAWS
FOR HEALTH

"And God looked upon the earth, and, behold, it was corrupt; for all flesh had corrupted his way upon the earth....and God said unto Noah....Behold, I will destroy them with the earth."

(Genesis 6:12-13)

Approximately one thousand years after God created man.....God said He was going to destroy His creation! Why? Because man "had corrupted (changed, 'to alter from the original' Webster) the way God intended man to live!!!

Listen to the Bible as it again talks about man changing the way God intended man to live.....only this time, it is after giving man a second chance. *"Professing themselves to be wise, they changed the truth of God into a lie, and worshipped and served the creature more than the creator.....and even as they did not like to retain God in their knowledge, God gave them over to a reprobate mind to do those things which are not convenient....."* (Romans 1:22, 25, 28)

GOD'S MORAL LAWS

Certainly, all Christians are aware of how man has rebelled against and broken the moral laws of God.

These moral laws are clearly set forth throughout the Old and New Testament of the Bible. They warn against murder, stealing, lying, cheating, sexual promiscuity, etc. But man rebelled against God's laws, went his own way and did his own thing. For these violations, man has paid a terrible price!

IGNORANCE OF GOD'S NATURAL LAWS

Most Christians are aware of and try to observe God's moral laws but what about God's natural laws— the laws of physics and chemistry? To most Christians, this is an unfamiliar area! Why? Because Christianity has devoted itself almost entirely to the spiritual side of man, while ignoring the physical side! Yet the Bible clearly teaches that man is a truine being....comprised of a spirit, soul and body!!! *"I pray God your whole spirit and soul and body be preserved blameless unto the coming of the Lord Jesus Christ."* (I Thessalonians 5:23)

Why Christians, even preachers, have ignored and even rejected God's natural laws, I don't know. But what I do know is that these laws are real and violators of these laws....whether Christians or non-Christians....will pay a terrible price for these violations in needless pain, suffering and premature death!

PERSONAL TESTIMONY

In previous chapters I spoke about physical changes I experienced as I applied God's natural laws to my own body.....changes that were almost unbelievable and would be considered miracles by those not familiar with the way the body functions.

Let me share a few of these changes that I personally experienced when I changed my diet and life-style.

1. My cancer either went away or went into remission.....After seventeen years I am not about to go to

the medical profession to find out which!

2. My blood pressure dropped from 150/90 to 110/70!

3. My pulse rate dropped from the low 70's to the upper 40's at rest!

4. My allergies departed! These allergies has been so severe at certain times of the year that I could not preach many a sermon without medication.

5. My sinuses cleared up!

6. My eyesight improved! I still have a pair of prescription glasses over twenty years old that are too strong!

7. My body odor and dandruff problems just up and left me!

8. Hemorrhoids which often required medication, went away!

9. Since 1976, when I started applying God's natural laws, I have not had a cold, an upset stomach, the flu, a headache, indigestion, constipation, or any other physical problem! To God be the glory!!! His natural laws and ways of living work!!!

10. My physical capabilities have improved spectacularly.....my physical endurance is boundless! At age 42 I would be out of breath from just climbing a flight of stairs. Now, seventeen years later, I can literally run up mountains!!!

You may want to reject what this book is teaching, but you cannot deny that the teachings of this book worked when I applied them to my body and life!!!

WHAT ARE THESE NATURAL LAWS?

What changes did I make in my life-style in 1976 that brought about these physical changes in my body and in my health? What are the natural laws which God established to keep man well and that would heal man's physical problems if the violations were stopped before man was drugged, burned, mutilated or died?

To answer these questions, we have to go back to creation and see what God told man and into what kind of environment God placed man.....and we have to assume that the way God taught man to live in the beginning was the way God intended man to live always! *"For I am the Lord, I change not."* (Malachi 3:6)

LET'S TAKE AN EXAMPLE

Let's take an example.....After God created man, *"The Lord God took man, and put him in the garden..... to dress it and it keep it."* (Genesis 2:15) Then, after man had sinned, *"The Lord God sent him forth from the Garden of Eden to till the ground...."* (Genesis 3:23)

Here is what I am getting at.....the further man removes himself from the way God intended man to live, the more likelihood there is that man will experience problems!!! Thus, rural living is closer to God's plan for man than suburban living! While urban (city) living is even further removed from God's plan than suburban living!

Most readers will agree with me, that there is a greater feeling of closeness to our Creator while walking down a country lane, walking through the woods, or while working in the garden than there is in the concrete jungle of the city with its polluted air, polluted water, traffic jams, noise, crime, rapid pace of life, etc.!

God intended man to live close to the earth so that man could *"Till the ground from whence he was taken"* (Genesis 3:23) *"And the Lord God planted a garden eastward in Eden; and there he put the man whom he had formed."* (Genesis 2:8)

MAN SHOULD LIVE TO BE 120 YEARS OLD

If we want a healthy, happy, physically active life, free from sickness and disease, right up until death (at about 120 years barring an accident or the Lord's return), we must try and make these natural laws a part of our lives!!! The closer we observe them, the greater we will be rewarded with superior health and a longer life!!! As to length of life, following the flood, God said, *"His days shall be an hundred and twenty years."* (Genesis 6:3)

For the rest of this chapter let's apply either the implied teachings of the Bible, the direct and clear teaching of the Bible or the practical experiences and scientific knowledge of today to find out what God's natural laws of health are.

I. PURE AIR

What kind of air would you expect to find in the Garden of Eden? Probably the best word to describe it would be "pure air", loaded with life-giving oxygen being given off by the plants and trees in the garden!

The greatest need of the body is "pure air"!!! Approximately 96% of our nutritional needs comes from the air! Thus the purer the air, the higher the quality of nourishment!

If we want to experience superior health, we must avoid polluted air!!! The greater the pollution, the greater the harm to the body!!! If you smoke.....stop!!! Shun smoke-filled rooms or any enclosed area with polluted air!!!

If you live in a city with poor air quality, consider a move to an area outside of the city and away from the pollution. Whatever changes are necessary in order to have fresh, pure air to breathe ought to receive serious consideration! Your health and very life depend on an abundant supply of pure air!!!

II. PURE WATER

Did God provide water for His creation? Yes! *"And a river went out of Eden to water the garden."* (Genesis 2:10)

What kind of water did God provide? It would have to be best described as "pure water"! Certainly the rivers were not polluted immediately after creation!

In Revelation 22:1 the Bible even describes the kind of water our heavenly home will have.....*"And he showed me a pure river of water of life, clear as crystal....."*

Today, man has so polluted the earth, that it is almost impossible to find a source of "pure water." Even rain water picks up so many pollutants as it falls through the atmosphere that it is anything but pure by the time it reaches the ground.

Probably the best way to obtain PURE WATER today is to purify your own drinking water right in your own home. Since 1976, I have been purifying the water in my home with a stainless steel, steam water distiller. It does require an initial investment, but if we want our bodies and those of our family to be healthy, we must put only "pure water" into them!

The body uses water to cleanse and remove toxins, to lubricate, to cool the body when overheated, etc. In fact, the body is comprised of from 75% to 85% water!

For the proper functioning of the body to maintain health, to cleanse, or to heal, the body must have pure water!!!

III. PURE LIVING FOOD

"And out of the ground made the Lord God to grow every tree that is pleasant to the sight, and good for food....." (Genesis 2:9)

"And God said, behold, I have given you every herb bearing seed (vegetables), which is upon the face of the earth, and every tree, in the which is the fruit of a tree yielding seed; to you it shall be for meat." (Genesis 1:29)

Food comprises only about four percent of the nutritional needs of the body! Yet without the right kinds of food prepared in the right manner the body is incapable of building strong, healthy, vital, vibrant cells and maintaining the body in superior health!!!

Eating the wrong kinds of foods or foods prepared in the wrong manner can create havoc in the body, clog up the body and cause all kinds of physical problems!

So let's see what we can learn about the food God intended man to eat:

1. ALL MEN, FROM ADAM TO NOAH, WERE VEGETARIANS AND FRUITARIANS!!! In Genesis 1:29, God said in substance: *"Fruits and vegetables, seeds, grains and nuts; to you it shall be for food."* On this meatless diet man lived an average of 912 years without a single recorded instance of sickness! You might find it interesting to read the first five chapters of Genesis in this regard.

2. MEAT WAS NOT CONSUMED BY MAN FOR OVER 1000 YEARS AFTER CREATION!!! It wasn't until after the flood, when all vegetation had been destroyed by water, that man began to eat meat! See Genesis 9:3. It is interesting to note that after man began eating meat, it took only a few generations for man's life span to drop from over 900 years to about 100. Genesis Chapter Eleven shows this rapid decline in life span very vividly. The life span of man then continued to decline to about 70 years.

3. FOOD WAS EATEN IN ITS WHOLE, NATURAL, LIVING, RAW STATE!!! There is not one indication in the Bible that for the first 1000 years after creation man cooked his food! Certainly they did not have gas or electric ranges or microwave ovens!

4. FOOD WAS NOT PROCESSED, PACKAGED, CANNED, FROZEN OR IRRADIATED!!! Nor were any chemical preservatives, coloring agents, flavor enhancers, growth hormones, antibotics, etc. added!

5. THIS FOOD WAS GROWN ORGANICALLY!!! There were no chemical fertilizers, pesticides, herbicides or fungacides used on the plants or applied to the ground!

IN SUMMARY:

MAN'S ORIGINAL DIET CONSISTED OF:
RAW VEGETABLES
RAW FRUITS
UNCOOKED SEEDS, GRAINS AND NUTS
which had been grown without any chemical poisons!!! This food was eaten in its whole, raw, living state without cooking, processing or additives.!!!

Does this sound like the kind of food and the way the average person consumes his food today? Today, by the time food is put into our mouth, it bears little resemblance to the "real thing"!

The question is not "Where's the beef?" The question is "Where is the food?" "Where is the nutrition?" "What has man done to the natural, wholesome food God created and intended man to eat?"

We have a body comprised of trillions of living cells! Living cells cannot be nourished with dead food!!! Life begets life!!! All cooked food is dead food!!! The heat of cooking destroys all of the enzymes, over 80% of the vitamins, changes the protein to an unusable form, and the organic minerals revert back to their inorganic state!!!

Tests conducted on raw eaters reveal that when cooked food is consumed, it actually causes the white blood cells to multiply in order to deal with this toxic, foreign substance entering the body!

That man is supposed to eat his food raw may be the most difficult thing to accept in this book because cooking of food has been practiced for thousands of years. It is a habit!!! Most of the human race is addicted to cooked food!!!

Yet man is the only member of the animal kingdom that cooks his food! Also, except where man has tampered with the food of the animal kingdom, sickness is practically non-existent!

In comparatively recent years, remote tribes have been found. They had been separated from the rest of the world for thousands of years, and yet they were found practically free from sickness and disease. When they started eating the processed, devitalized, foods of modern man they began having problems similar to the "so called" civilized world!

Today, if man wants to experience superior health and avoid sickness and disease, he must consume his food in a state just as close as it can be to the way God created it and intended man to consume it...without processing, additives, or heat....and grown organically!!!

IV. VIGOROUS EXERCISE

God created man to be physically active because He put man into a garden setting that required physical exertion in order to sustain life! In Genesis 2:15, God said man was to *"dress and keep"* the garden. Genesis 3:19 says that in order to *"dress and keep"* the garden it would require *"the sweat of the face."* Genesis 3:23 says man was to *"till the ground."*

When God created man, He created him so that physical activity would be necessary in order for man to obtain his food, and that the physical activity necessary to obtain his food would be vigorous enough to cause him to sweat. The Bible even says *"....that if any would not work, neither should he eat."* (II Thessalonians 3:10)

It is only in recent years that we have learned that daily physical exercise is an absolute imperative to maintaining a healthy body!!! Yet man still seems to pride himself on how much physical work he can escape.

For the body to function properly and in order to experience superior health, daily, vigorous physical exercise is an absolute necessity!!!

V. ABUNDANT SUNSHINE

God created man to live his life mostly in the great-out-of-doors where the body could receive abundant sunshine!!! In fact, man was created and placed in the garden so attired that the sun would shine upon his entire body! *"And they were both naked, the man and his wife, and were not ashamed."* (Genesis 2:25)

Today the majority of people spend most of their lives indoors with possibly an occasional weekend or vacation outdoors.

Granted, due to the depletion of the ozone layer, there is the possibility of getting an excess of the harmful rays.....but this is usually a problem only in the hotter climates during the hottest times of the day and year.

However, the body cannot function properly without sunshine!!! All of God's creation is dependent on the sun for life! The sun is man's best source of vitamin "D"! The sun makes it possible for the body to assimilate calcium! The sun supplies the body with energy! The sun warms and soothes the body!

Man needs to spend as much time in the out-of-doors in the fresh air and sunshine as is possible, exposing as much of the body to its healing, soothing rays as is practical and modest for the situation! (Warning: If you have not been getting much sun, be careful not to expose yourself to too much sun at one time....and be sure to avoid sunburn!)

VI. ADEQUATE REST

"The sleep of a labouring man is sweet, whether he eat little or much: but the abundance of the rich will not suffer him to sleep." (Ecclesiastes 5:12)

The person who labours physically during the day will usually have little trouble going to sleep, and his sleep will usually be a sound sleep. However, the person who has little physical activity will often experience difficulty getting to sleep and often not experience sound sleep. Without daily, vigorous, physical activity, the body just doesn't function properly!!!

The purpose of sleep is so the body will have time to cleanse itself, recharge itself with energy for the next day's activities and to repair and rebuild its cells!

The average person spends about one-third of his life in sleep.

Sleep should be enjoyed! It should be in a quiet place! It should take place where there is an abundance of fresh pure air! The best place to sleep is outdoors, so the closer we can duplicate that condition, the better! Leaving the window open during sleep would be one suggestion.

As a person observes the natural laws set forth in this chapter, his need for sleep usually decreases significantly! This is due to the cleaner body requiring less time to cleanse and rebuild and recharge itself! The quality of sleep a person experiences is often a good indicator of his physical, mental and emotional well being!

VII. POSTIVE THINKING

"A merry heart doeth good like a medicine: but a broken spirit drieth the bones." (Proverbs 17:22)

Thousands of years ago the Bible told us there was a relationship between our thoughts and emotions and the condition of the body. Today we have conclusive evidence that many illnesses are the result of our negative thinking and unstable emotions!

Negative thinking has a wearing down effect on the physical body. Negative emotions can actually bring about physical problems!!! Negative thinking is one of the reasons **"Why Christians Get Sick"**!

Positive thinking and a positive outlook on life are necessary ingredients for a healthy, happy, successful life!!!

TODAY'S SOCIETY

The world in which we live today is very different from the world into which God placed the first family! Adam and Eve had a slow-paced life with few pressures and with lots of physical activity! There were no eight-to-five jobs, 'moonlighting' jobs, or jobs that required hours of hectic travel. There were no electric bills, telephone bills, car payments, mortgage payments or credit card payments due each month! There were no radios, televisions or telephones to disrupt their lives; no traffic jams or sirens!

No, they were in a gorgeous setting, surrounded with beautiful trees, flowers and vegetables along with the beautiful singing of birds, gurgling water in the brooks, the rustling of leaves and the singing of the wind in the trees!

The pace of life today is too fast.....too hectic!!! Many people drive themselves to keep up with the 'Joneses', or to have the so-called, "necessities" or nicer things of life.

God meant life to be very simple, basic, and beautiful as man walked in closeness to God's creation! But man has made life very different and a lot more difficult than God ever intended! Man has corrupted God's ways!!! Man has changed the way God intended man to live!!!

I have met many people living with an abundance of material things who were miserable and unhappy, while others who may have had little of this world's goods were living a full and happy life close to nature! *"But godliness with contentment is great gain. For we brought nothing into this world, and it is certain we can carry nothing out. And having food and raiment let us be therewith content."* (I Timothy 6:6-8)

CONCLUDING WORDS

Sickness and disease and physical problems are not normal!!! They are the penalty one pays for violating God's natural laws!!!

God intended man to enjoy life.....*"I am come that they might have life, and that they might have it more abundantly."* (John 10:10)

God also wants us to be healthy.....*"Beloved, I wish above all things that thou mayest prosper and be in health even as thy soul prospereth."* (III John 2)

It is very difficult to enjoy life or anything else if you do not have your health!!!

God provided a way to a healthy, happy, spiritual life!!! Now it is up to each one of us to accept God's abundant provision. *"If ye know these things, happy are ye if ye do them."* (John 13:17)

CHAPTER TEN — IN REVIEW

The best way to review Chapter Ten.....is to re-read "GOD'S NATURAL LAWS." They hold the key to your health, happiness, future, and very life!!!

11

IT'S TIME TO DO SOMETHING ABOUT IT!!!!!

".....I have set before you life and death, blessing and cursing: therefore choose life, that both thou and thy seed may live."

(Deuteronomy 30:19)

While writing Chapter Ten of this book, I received two letters that distressed me very greatly....and yet they so clearly reveal the importance of this book and the urgency of getting it into the hands of all Christians.

The first letter was from my sister, Carolyn -

"Dear George,
I have the most terrible news anyone could ever have in their life.....my Sweetheart died of cancer. He was only 52.....We loved each other so much..... We had our new home, and we were so happy..... Around August, he began to act very odd. He had been such a sweet and gentle man! He became violent toward things....and verbally abusive to almost anyone in sight, especially me....I was in shock.....I was at a total loss.....I couldn't begin to imagine what had come over him. I never dreamed of physical illness — he had a hernia operation July 10th and they said he was fine.....In Septem-

ber he developed "sciatica" in his left leg.....Soon after, a pain in his left shoulder....Then, on Sept. 20, his left collar bone broke! Just **broke** during the night! At the emergency room they told us to see a doctor the next day. He went into the hospital....On the 26th, they told us he had cancer..... 'the bad kind.' They told me, 'one year at the most.' Okay. We were ready to fight and do anything to prove them wrong. But we never had a chance. He had chemotherapy and radiation therapy....The pain was horrendous. It was heartbreaking. He was so brave. My emotional pain matched his physical pain.....I treated him like a precious flower. He became so delicate — just a skeleton. He was so dear. He would yell at me.....in my eagerness to help him, sometimes I was too rough, but then, instantly he would say, 'I'm sorry. Don't pay any attention to me. I love you so much. you know I do'.....He was so sweet.....I would have done anything on earth to help him. I never let him lose hope that he would get better.....On the night before he died some man came in to see him and was praying over him as if he was going to die any minute. Frank opened his eyes and said, loud and clear, 'Wait a minute. I have other options! I'm getting **TREATMENTS,** you know!' He believed and so did I. That night he was up and around. For the first time he waved to me from his window when I left the hospital. The next morning I arrived bright and early with the suitcase — he was coming home!.....But he was in a coma and never came out of it. His feet had turned black and his hands were beginning to. I've never known how absolutely devastating cancer is. If only he could have just had one hour again, when he felt good and we could talk. But he never did from the time we found out. I would have given anything for that.....Life and love are so precious. But there's no way to truly understand how precious they are until you feel them slipping away forever.

This is the most frustrating experience imaginable. I miss him terribly and want him back! But everywhere I turn, the door is closed and locked forever. He was so good. He didn't deserve this. We didn't. Why him George! Can you tell me?..... Why did God do this to us? Please write to me."

HOW WOULD YOU ANSWER THIS LETTER???

Here is part of my answer -

"I just got your letter a few minutes ago. Tears streamed down my face as I read it. I wanted so much to be able to somehow reach out to you and try to comfort you in your great loss and pain. Life seems so unfair sometimes. Is there any way you could come down for a visit?.....

Carolyn, God **was not** to blame for what happened to Frank. In fact, the book I am writing contains the answers you are seeking as to why. The title of the book is: **'Why Christians Get Sick'**, and tells why Mom and Frank had cancer and why Dad had his heart attacks and strokes. I'm going to go into town in a few minutes and have copies made of the book and send it to you. This is just a rough draft, and it is not finished, but I pray you will find it helpful....."

MY BIRTHDAY GIRL DIES

Just a few days after receiving the above letter from my sister, I received the following -

"Your birthday girl, Susanna, went home to be with Jesus December 15, after major surgery."

Susanna was the daughter of a young couple who met and courted in the church. I married them. They later went on to Bible College and have been pastoring their own church for many years.

When their first child, Susanna, was born, her birthday was on February 12, the same date as mine. Because of this, Susanna has always been extra special to me!

Now this beautiful 14-year-old girl was gone! The reason?.....in talking to Susanna's mom and dad, I learned it was because of an unsuccessful operation to remove a tumor that was pressing on her spinal column!

SOME CANCER STATISTICS

1. CANCER IS NOW KILLING MORE CHILDREN BETWEEN THE AGES OF 3-14 THAN ANYTHING ELSE!

2. ONE OUT OF EVERY THREE AMERICANS WILL DEVELOP CANCER DURING THEIR LIFETIME, AND THIS **INCLUDES CHRISTIANS!**

3. ONE OUT OF EVERY FIVE DEATHS IN AMERICA IS NOW CAUSED BY CANCER!

4. TWO OUT OF EVERY THREE FAMILIES IN AMERICA WILL HAVE A MEMBER SUFFER THE RAVAGES OF CANCER!

5. EACH YEAR, APPROXIMATELY 500,000 AMERICANS DIE FROM CANCER!!!!!

6. WHAT IS THE COST TO THE AMERICAN PEOPLE FOR CANCER TREATMENT..... **OVER $100,000,000,000 EACH YEAR!!!!!**

SURGERY, CHEMOTHERAPY AND RADIATION

Dr. Mary Ruth Swope in her excellent book, **"Green Leaves of Barley"** states: "The uselessness of surgery for cancer has been known for at least three decades. Your surgeon, of course, will be the last to admit it. As long as he can find people to submit to his scalpel, he will! But, it is well known in medical circles that surgery causes cancer cells to spread.

Doctors at Kaiser Hospital in California have shown radiation to cause new cancers to form where the x-rays of the first radiation burns normal tissue..... chemotherapy, too, is not as effective as we have been taught to believe.....while it destroys cancer cells in the blood, it also damages healthy cells and generally weakens the immune system."

"If Americans want to get well from cancer, heart disease, arthritis, diabetes, obesity, and a whole host of debilitating conditions, in my opinion, they will have to find nonorthodox treatment modalities involving nutrition and other remedies "provided by nature" as the major components."

"We can't expect the medical community to inform us of "natural remedies" of which they themselves are ignorant."

(Dr. Swope has served on the Foods and Nutrition faculty at Purdue University.....later served as Head of Foods and Nutrition at the University of Nevada..... Head of Home Economics at Queens College and Dean of the School of Home Economics, Eastern Illinois University.)

CANCER RESEARCH

After spending billions of dollars on cancer research, the number of people developing and dying of cancer continues to increase!!! Deaths from cancer rose 223% from 1960 to 1982!!!

Recently, the American Cancer Society has told us that research indicates an improved diet may be helpful in keeping a person from developing cancer..... They make the following recommendations:

1. EAT MORE HIGH-FIBER FOODS SUCH AS FRUIT, VEGETABLES AND WHOLE CEREALS.
2. INCLUDE DARK GREEN AND DEEP YELLOW FRUITS AND VEGETABLES RICH IN

VITAMINS "A" AND "C".
3. INCLUDE BROCCOLI, CABBAGE, BRUS-SEL SPROUTS, KOHLRABI, AND CAULI-FLOWER.
4. BE MODERATE IN CONSUMPTION OF SALT-CURED, SMOKED, AND NITRITE-CURED FOODS.
5. CUT DOWN ON TOTAL FAT INTAKE FROM ANIMAL SOURCES AND FATS AND OILS.
6. AVOID OBESITY.
7. BE MODERATE IN CONSUMPTION OF AL-COHOLIC BEVERAGES.

HEART ATTACKS

Heart disease is the cause of one out of every two deaths in America...**OVER 1,000,000 (ONE MILLION) PERSONS EACH YEAR!!!** The cost to the American people...**OVER $7,000,000,000 (SEVEN BILLION DOLLARS) ANNUALLY!!!**

Recent statistics indicate a slight decline in the percentage of deaths caused by heart attacks. We are told that the reason for the slight decrease is improved diet!

I find this all very interesting! Why??? Because the "authorities" have been telling us for years that what we eat has nothing to do with our physical well being and now they are advising that a change in our diet will help reduce the risk of cancer and heart attacks!!!

DIETARY GOALS FOR THE UNTIED STATES

In 1977, the UNITED STATES SENATE issued "DIETARY GOALS FOR THE UNITED STATES." In the "Forward" of this report, Senator George McGovern, Chairman of the Select Committee on Nutrition and Human Needs said, "The purpose of this report is to point out that the eating patterns of this century represent as critical a public concern as any now before us."

Senator Charles H. Percy, Ranking Minority Member, said, "Without government and industry committment to good nutrition, the American people will continue to eat themselves to poor health."

The "goals" of the report "suggest the following changes in food selection and preparation":

1. INCREASE CONSUMPTION OF FRUITS AND VEGETABLES AND WHOLE GRAINS.

2. DECREASE CONSUMPITON OF MEAT AND INCREASE CONSUMPTION OF POULTRY AND FISH.

3. DECREASE CONSUMPTION OF FOODS HIGH IN FAT AND PARTIALLY SUBSTITUTE POLY-UNSATURATED FAT FOR SATURATED FAT.

4. SUBSTITUTE NON-FAT MILK FOR WHOLE MILK.

5. DECREASE CONSUMPTION OF BUTTERFAT, EGGS AND OTHER HIGH CHOLESTEROL SOURCES.

6. DECREASE CONSUMPTION OF SUGAR AND FOODS HIGH IN SUGAR CONTENT.

7. DECREASE CONSUMPTION OF SALT AND FOODS HIGH IN SALT CONTENT.

STATEMENT OF SENATOR GEORGE McGOVERN ON THE PUBLICATION OF DIETARY GOALS FOR THE UNITED STATES (Press Conference, Friday, January 14, 1977, Room 457, Dirksen Senate Office Building)

"Good morning.

The purpose of this press conference is to release a nutrition committee study entitled **Dietary Goals for the United States,** and to explain why we need such a report.

I should note from the outset that this is the first comprehensive statement by any branch of the Federal government on risk factors in the American diet.

The simple fact is that our diets have changed radically within the last 50 years, with great and often very harmful effects on our health. These dietary changes represent as great a threat to public health as smoking. Too much fat, too much sugar and salt, can be and are linked directly to heart disease, cancer, obesity, and stroke, among other killer diseases. In all, six of the ten leading causes of death in the United States have been linked to our diet.

Those of us within government have an obligation to acknowledge this. The public wants some guidance, wants to know the truth, and hopefully today we can lay the cornerstone for the building of better health for all Americans, through better nutrition....."

STATEMENT OF DR. D. M. HEGSTED, PROFESSOR OF NUTRITION, HARVARD SCHOOL OF PUBLIC HEALTH, BOSTON, MASS. (Press Conference, Friday, January 14, 1977, Room 457, Dirkson Senate Office Building)

"The diet of the American people has become increasingly rich—rich in meat, other sources of saturated fat and cholesterol, and in sugar.....It should be emphasized that this diet which affluent people generally consume is everywhere associated with a similar disease pattern—high rates of ischemic heart disease, certain forms of cancer, diabetes, and obesity. These are the major causes of death and disability in the United States....."

Ischemic heart disease, cancer, diabetes and hypertension are the diseases that kill us. They are epidemic in our population. We cannot afford to temporize. We have an obligation to inform the public of the current state of knowledge and to assist the public in making the correct food choices. To do less is to avoid our responsibility."

STATEMENT OF DR. BEVERLY WINIKOFF, ROCKEFELLER FOUNDATION, NEW YORK, N.Y. (Press Conference, Friday, January 14, 1977, Room 457, Dirkson Senate Office Building)

".....There is a widespread and unfounded confidence in the ability of medical science to cure or mitigate the effects of such diseases once they occur. Appropriate public education must emphasize the unfortunate but clear limitations of current medical practice in curing the common killer diseases. Once hypertension, diabetes, arteriosclerosis or heart disease are manifest, there is, in reality, very little that medical science can do to return a patient to normal physiological function. As awareness of this limitation increases, the importance of prevention will become all the more obvious."

STATEMENT OF DR. PHILIP LEE, PROFESSOR OF SOCIAL MEDICINE AND DIRECTOR, HEALTH POLICY PROGRAM, UNIVERSITY OF CALIFORNIA, SAN FRANCISCO, CALIF. (Press Conference, Friday, January 14, 1977, Room 457, Dirksen Senate Office Building)

".....As a nation we have come to believe that medicine and medical technology can solve our major health problems. The role of such important factors as diet in cancer and heart disease has long been obscured by the emphasis on the conquest of these diseases through the miracles of modern medicine. Treatment not prevention, has been the order of the day. The problem can never be solved merely by more and more medical care.....Finally, our greatest bulwark against the interests that have helped to create the present problems is an informed public."

THE DIET OF CHRISTIANS

For some reason, the average Christian, or for that matter, the average American, has given little thought in the past to what they put into their bodies. Part of this lack of concern can probably be traced to faith in the "food industry", believing that they would not produce or market a product that could be harmful, believing also that the Government agencies set up for just such a purpose would protect them from harmful products.

AMERICAN MEDICAL ASSOCIATION

However, I believe the American Medical Association has to shoulder major blame for the citizen's lack of concern. Their failure to warn the people of the dangers in the average American diet becomes quite understandable when one realizes that of the 127 medical schools in the United States, only one-third even offer a course on nutrition, and that only one-half of that one-third require attendance!!!

When the "DIETARY GOALS FOR THE UNITED STATES" were published in 1977, the American Medical Association in an April 18, 1977, letter, to the Nutrition Committee states, "The evidence for assuming that benefits to be derived from the adoption of such universal goals as set forth in the report is not conclusive and.....potential for harmful effects... would occur through adoption of the proposed national goals."

Before the end of 1977, the first Edition of **"Dietary Goals for the United States"** was no longer available and had been replaced with a second edition!!! The second edition was published in December 1977 and contained a three page forward quoting the American Medical Association who said that to change your diet may be harmful!!! The forward then goes on, attempting to discredit the entire document by saying that science has not proven any connection between diet and disease!!!

Remember, this is all coming from the **'experts',** the people who are supposed to teach and protect the citizenry, in fact, they, along with the "American

Dietetic Association" (ADA), are the only ones legally able to do so as the laws presently stand!!!

AMERICAN DIETETIC ASSOCIATION

And speaking of the American Dietetic Association whose members do have the legal right and responsibility to tell the American people what they should and should not eat....and what constitutes a 'balanced diet'.....we find that their teachings are LUDICROUS ('...meriting derisive laughter or scorn as absurdly inept, false, or foolish' Webster)!!!

To find a good example of the "ADA's" teachings, check out the meals being served at your local hospital.....meals prepared by ADA-approved dieticians. An analysis of these meals will quickly reveal that they are so poor nutritionally, they would contribute more to a person remaining in the hospital than helping them get well and be able to return to their homes!!!

Check out the average school lunch program for another vivid example of an ADA approved menu — pizza, greasy foods (hamburgers, French fries, etc.) hot dogs, and sugar desserts are just a few examples of the typical menu. And remember, this is coming from the 'experts' who are supposed to be showing the American people what constitutes a wholesome diet!!!

IF I SEEM HARSH

If I seem harsh in some of the things I have written, please forgive me! I only want Christians to be aware of the situation! However, neither Christians nor the American people will realize what is happening to them unless someone tells them and warns them!!!

If I have come down hard on the medical profession or the ADA, I am not denouncing any particular individual. Most are sincerely trying to help their fellow man! However, no matter how sincere, they are wrong in their whole approach to nutrition, health and healing!!!

Thank God, He showed me the error of the teachings and methods used by these groups. But it is an outrage when Christians follow their pernicious teachings and allow them to drug, burn and mutilate the bodies of Christians!!! Bodies that are the "Temples of God!!!"

CHRISITAN SCHOOLS

For many years Christians sat idly by and allowed a secular, humanistic educational system to remove God, the Bible, prayer and the teachings of morality from the classrooms of our public schools, while teaching that man descended from a monkey.

When the Christian community was sufficiently outraged, Christians did something about it....and thus the Christian School movement was born! This movement peaked during the late nineteen-seventies, at which time a brand new Christian School was opening its doors every day! Today, in almost every community in America, Christian parents have an alternative educational system to offer their children! Praise the Lord!!!

HEALING PROFESSIONS

For too many years Christians have sat idly by while the world took total control of the healing professions as well as the bodies of Christians, which are God's temples!!!

Christians take their sick to doctors and hospitals where the entire approach to healing and health are mostly in direct opposition to God's Ways!!! Christians have allowed their bodies to be drugged by chemicals, burned by radiation and mutilated by removing the unhealthy body parts through surgery!

When the patient doesn't get well, or dies, the Christian accepts "we did all that we could" as a valid explanation from the medical profession and then spiritually rationalizes it by saying it was "God's will!"

It is high time that Christians realized that the medical profession's failures are not necessarily "God's will", nor has the medical profession done all that could be done!!!

HIPPOCRATES

Hippocrates, the great physician of the Fifth Century BC is called the "Father of Medicine". He said, "Where there is love for mankind, there is the love for the art of healing."

This great physician taught that food must be taken in the condition it is found in nature. Uncooked!!! He further taught, "Your food shall be your medicine" and "Your medicine shall be your food."

It is sad that the medical profession has deviated so far from the principles laid down by its founder!!!

WHAT CAN CHRISTIANS DO???

1. **START** — Taking steps to improve your own health will be an excellent start! The natural laws found in Chapter Ten contain the ingredients for you personally to experience superior health!

2. **CHANGE YOUR THINKING** — Christians, including pastors, evangelists and missionaries, need to change their thinking concerning sickness and health! They need to start questioning whether their present diet and life style will produce sickness or superior health! A mind open to new thoughts is an absolute necessity if superior health is to be obtained! It is not easy to change lifelong thinking patterns! Ask the Lord to help you!!!

3. **EDUCATION** — Christians must re-educate themselves! Knowledge is absolutely necessary in order to make intelligent changes! There are many excellent books available. We must stop accepting as "Gospel" all that the "so-called" experts are telling us! Remember that were there

no sickness, the "experts" would be out of business!!!

4. **TEACH** — In the churches, pastors and Sunday School teachers must include in their teachings, the proper care of the body, "God's Temple!" Our Christian schools and colleges must offer courses that teach the biblical approach to the care of the body, and curriculum must be developed for the classrooms!

5. **CHANGE THE LAWS** — The "American Medical Association" and the "American Dietetic Association" have a stranglehold on the healing arts! (A parent whose child develops cancer can have the child legally taken away from him if he won't subject the child to the drugs, burning and mutilation of the medical profession!) The ADA is presently trying to get every other field that offers nutritional advice banned by law...and that would even prevent churches from teaching a healthy diet! It is presently a criminal offense to offer advice to a sick person unless you are a member of their elite associations! Present laws allow medical doctors to drug, burn, and even mutilate bodies, and even if the patient dies as a result of these barbaric efforts, it is legal!!! Find out what the laws are in your state. Write to your Representatives telling of your concern! Send them a copy of this book! Because of current laws, Americans have to go to a foreign country if they want an alternative to the drugging, burning and cutting...These laws must be changed!!!

6. **HOSPITALS** — Churches must start their own "Healing Retreats" where Christians with physical problems can be offered healing methods that are consistent with God's teachings! As the Christian school movement spread across the nation--when churches opened their own schools, so must "Temple Retreats" be established!!!

7. **DOCTORS** — These "Temple Retreats" must be staffed by nutritional doctors and nurses who have been trained in the natural healing arts! Christian colleges must provide these courses and degrees!!!

8. **HOSPITALIZATION INSURANCE** — The insurance industry must extend its coverage to include alternative methods of healing! This would result in tremendous savings to the industry as well as lower rates for the people!

9. **ORGANIC FOOD** — Christians must start demanding that their produce departments and markets carry produce raised without chemicals!!! If millions of Americans would make this demand, the pressure exerted on the food industry would make it happen!!! Already in California and some other states, some food markets are starting to specialize in organically grown food. Germany has super market chains presently doing this!

10. **GROW YOUR OWN FOOD** — Every Christian who has the smallest piece of ground needs to have a garden! It is amazing but true that a garden of only 200 sq. ft. with a six month growing season can grow the yearly amount of vegetables consumed by the average American! Organic growing methods must be taught in our churches and schools! We must get back to the land and grow our food as God intended it to be grown!!! Through the growing of sprouts, the average kitchen window can be turned into an indoor garden where organic food can be grown all year long!

11. **ORGANIC FARMS** — In close proximity to every city in America, we need enterpreneurs who will develop organic farms to provide chemical-free produce for those who cannot grow their own! In colder climates, the use of greenhouses could

make year-round production possible. Granted, produce costs would increase, but this would be more than off-set by better health.....and money saved that is presently spent on non-food items and medical bills!

12. **WE MUST SHARE OUR KNOWLEDGE, BURDEN AND ENTHUSIASM CONCERNING THE PROPER CARE OF THE BODY WITH FAMILY, FRIENDS AND NEIGHBORS!!!** This book can be a tremendous tool to put into their hands! Especially must we get this book and knowledge into the hands of pastors, evangelists, missionaries, Christian school leaders and other Christian leaders who have influence over multitudes!

SOME CONCLUDING WORDS

The food presently being consumed and the life style that is being followed is slowly destroying the health and vitality of our great nation, including the Christian community! Various forms of sickness and disease are consuming a larger and larger part of our energy, time, money, and emotions!

Why is this happening? Because we have gotten on the wrong road concerning health, nutrition, and the proper care of the body! *"...For wide is the gate, and broad is the way, that leadeth to destruction, and many there be which go in thereat: because straight is the gate, and narrow is the way, which leadeth unto life, and few there be that find it."* (Matthew 7:13-14)

It is not necessary to continue down the road that leads to sickness, disease and an early grave!!! By changing our ways, giving up the bad ways and following the natural ways God has set forth, we can enjoy the wonderful blessings of superior health that our Creator intended to be our portion!!!

We must reject the life-destroying foods and habits that are destroying our bodies by refusing to partake of them any more!!! Old ways must pass away, behold, all things must become new with regard to diet and life style!!!

There is only one way to deal with our physical bodies, "God's Temple", and that is God's Way!!! His Ways are perfect!!! His Ways lead to superior health and a happy long life!!! May this be your portion!!!

"Beloved, I wish above all things that thou mayest prosper and be in health, even as thy soul prospereth." (III John 2) This is my prayer for you!!! May God abundantly bless you!!!

".....I have set before you life and death, blessing and cursing: therefore choose life, that both thou and thy seed may live:" (Deuteronomy 30:19)

"And Elijah came unto all the people, and said, how long halt ye between two opinions? If the Lord be God, follow him..." (I Kings 18:21)

12

CONCLUSION

"The Lord has done great things for us; whereof we are glad."

(Psalm 126:3)

The Lord has been very good to me! At the age of 23 He showed me the way of salvation. I accepted His invitation and received Jesus into my heart as my personal Saviour. By this time twenty-three years of my life had passed without personally knowing my Creator. But on May 29, 1957, the Great Creator became my Saviour!!!

Almost immediately I became concerned for others and began telling them about Jesus. It wasn't long before I was in school preparing for the ministry.

The Lord gave me many exciting and memorable years as pastor; pastoring four different churches, starting two new churches, a Christian school, Bible institute, fifteen years as a "radio pastor" with the "America Needs Christ" radio broadcast, and much more. But the most thrilling part of it all was the privilege of sharing Jesus with others; seeing multitudes come to know Jesus personally, along with their lives being changed in such marvelous ways.

During those years I often said when urged to slow down due to my zeal and total dedication, "I would rather burn out then rust out!"

But when at the age of 42 I found myself about to "burn out" (the prognosis for colon cancer is not very exciting), I just could not accept it as "God's will" for me and I started seeking answers. In Chapter One I shared some of these experiences.

Now, some Christians may question my emphasis on the "body" in this book, but I believe with all my heart that the Lord has shown me the things in this book and prepared me for a "Temple" ministry!

There are literally thousands of ministers helping to prepare people to die. But how many are teaching people how to live? How many are teaching people how to live a vibrantly healthy, abundantly happy life so that they will have the energy and health to share Christ, yea, even the health to remain alive to tell the good news?

POTENTIAL RAMIFICATIONS

My Christian friend, do you realize the potential ramifications of the information contained in this book if these teachings were applied universally???

1. Missionaries, pastors, evangelists and their families would not be forced to leave their fields of ministry due to sickness...or have their ministries ended prematurely by death!!!

2. Expensive doctor, hospital, and drug bills would be eliminated!!! In fact, the only need for doctors and hospitals would be to repair broken bodies caused by accidents!

3. Hospital visitation would practically become a thing of the past as there would be no sickness! Funerals would only take place when the elderly died from old age, or as the result of accidents!

4. Eventually, even nursing homes would become almost unnecessary, as the elderly would remain active, alert, and able to take care of themselves almost until death!

5. Through the teaching of proper nutrition and life style from the pulpits and through mis-

sionary outreach, world hunger could be over-come!

6. Many missionary societies have used medical missionaries not only to help third-world countries physically, but also as a means of reaching people with the Gospel. Think of the multitudes who could be reached for Jesus through a "Temple" ministry that not only made the people well, but kept them from getting sick!!! Missionaries could have a dual ministry, teaching people how to live, while preparing them for eternity!!!

MY PERSONAL COMMITMENT

For the past almost 20 years of my life, I have been asking the Lord to show me "WHY CHRISTIANS GET SICK." He has done that, and in so doing has also shown me how Christians can be well and experience superior health!

The more the Lord opened my eyes and revealed His natural laws concerning health to me, the more I wanted to share this knowledge with others!

Several years ago Dr. Al Janney, who was then president of the American Association of Christian Schools, asked me if I would be willing to set up a "Health Retreat" in Center Hill, Florida, where sick pastors, evangelists, missionaries, and Christian leaders could receive alternative health care.

Dr. Janney had the burden and the facilities but not the financing! He tried to get other pastors to support the project as a missionary outreach, but the project died for lack of interest.

It was then that I realized that before such a ministry could materialize, the Christian community had to be made aware of God's natural laws of health and the need of such a ministry!!!

For the past several years, I have been writing this book.....while at the same time, trying to place myself in a position where I could help others! I feel that I can best help others by writing books, producing tapes, giving lectures and seminars, evaluating products, providing demonstration organic gardens and orchards, teaching food preparation and storage methods, and of course by example!

After several years of struggle I have been able to situate myself on a 50 acre piece of mountain land here in northeast Tennessee, where there is pure air, chemical free soil, abundant springs, peaceful surroundings, organic gardens and orchards. It is called "HALLELUJAH ACRES", a place where the beauty of God's creation is so abundantly evident!

My goal is to make "Hallelujah Acres" into a modern "Garden of Eden," from which God's natural ways for healing and health will flow to Christians around the world!!!

Also, I envision "Hallelujah Acres" being a place where pastors, evangelists, missionaries and Christian leaders can come for seminars where they will learn first hand how to grow, prepare and serve foods as God intended. Nutrition and proper care of the body will be taught and then these Christian leaders can go back to their respective areas of influence to share this knowledge with others!!!

I personally believe the American people and especially Christians are thoroughly disenchanted with the present means available dealing with sickness, health and nutrition and are just waiting for someone to show them a better way!!!

I want to and am willing and ready to do all that I can to see this happen!!! Will you help me??? I cannot do it alone!!! The job is staggaring, but the potential rewards can be fabulously exciting!!!

If you are interested in helping, write me! Even a letter stating that you are standing with me in prayer would be encouraging and appreciated!

WOULD YOU LIKE TO RECEIVE
OUR FREE NEWSLETTER?

Our ministry has grown tremendously in the past few years, and Hallelujah Acres is now publishing an extremely informative quarterly newsletter, called *Back to the Garden.* **And subscriptions are free!** If you would like to receive this newsletter, just write:

Rev. George Malkmus
Hallelujah Acres
P.O. Box 10
Eidson, TN 37731

PASTOR / MISSIONARY PROJECT

Hallelujah Acres Ministries is establishing a "Pastor / Missionary Project" to place this book in the hands of as many pastors, evangelists, missionaries and Christian school leaders as possible. The goal is that eventually every Christian leader will have the information contained in this book! If you would like to help with this project, mark your gift, "Pastor / Missionary Project."

ARE YOU A CHRISTIAN?

Although this book is written for Christians, it is possible, dear reader, that you are not a true, Bible Christian. If not, please consider that you can apply all the principles of this book and live a long, healthy life, but spend eternity separated from God and heaven! If this is your case, God's good news is that the Lord Jesus Christ shed His sinless blood as the full, finished payment for sin, was buried and rose again for our justification. By placing our faith and trust in Him and His blood alone, we are saved, born from above, become a new creature in Christ and headed for an eternity in heaven! Will you place your faith in Christ now? (If you will, please write me, and I will send you more Biblical information to help you spiritually.)

BIBLIOGRAPHY

1. *ABC of the Human Body.* Pleasantville, N.Y.: The Reader's Digest Assoc. Inc., 1987.
2. Airola, Paavo, Ph.D., *Hypoglycemia: A Better Approach.* Phoenix: Health Plus, 1977.
3. _____ *Rejuvenation Secrets from Around the World.* Phoenix: Health Plus, 1977.
4. Allen, Hannan, *Homemakers Guide to Foods for Pleasure and Health.* Chicago: Natural Hygiene Press, Inc., 1976.
5. Berry, Linda, D.C., *Internal Cleansing.* Capitola, California: Botanica Press, 1985.
6. Boie, Thorwald and Shirley, *Raw Food Diet Plan.* Los Angeles: Boie Enterprises, 1971.
7. Bragg, Paul C., N.D., Pt. T., *Nerve Force.* Hot Springs, California: Health Science, 1975.
8. _____ *Internal Physical Fitness.* Hot Springs, California: Health Science.
9. _____ *Natures Way to Health:* Hot Springs, California: Health Science, 1979.
10. _____ *The Philosophy of Super-Health.* Hot Springs, California: Health Science, 1975.
11. _____ *The Shocking Truth About Water.* Hot Springs, California: Health Science, 1975.
12. Christopher, John R., M.H., *Dr. Christopoher's Three Day Cleansing Program and Mucusless Diet.* Springville, Utah: Dr. Christopher, 1969.
13. Cook, Lewis E. Jr. and Junko Yasui, *Goldot.* Yorktown, Texas: Life Science, 1978.
14. Diamond, Harvey and Marilyn, *Fit for Life.* New York: Warner Books, 1985.
15. _____ *Living Health.* New York: Warner Books, 1987.
16. Ehret, Arnold, Prof., *Mucusless Diet Healing System.* Beaumont, California: Ehret Literature Publishing Co., 1922.
17. Fathman, George and Doris, *Live Foods.* Beaumont, California: Ehret Literature Publishing Co., 1967.
18. Fry, T.C., *The Myth of Medicine.* Austin, Texas: Life Science, 1974.
19. _____ *The Miracle of Living Foods.* Austin, Texas: Life Science.
20. _____ *The Great Water Controversy.* Austin, Texas: LIfe Science, 1974.
21. Gray, Robert, *The Colon Health Handbook.* Oakland, California: Rockridge Publishing Co., 1982.
22. Heritage, Ford, *Composition and Facts About Food.* Mokelumne Hill, California: Health Research, 1968.
23. Hoffman, Debbie L., *The Raw Food Program.* Valley Center, California: Professional Press, 1984.
24. Havannessian, Arshavir Ter, *Raw Eating.* Tehran, Iran: Arshavir Ter Hovannessian, 1967.
25. Hunter, Beatrice Trum, *Food Additives and Your Health.* New Cannon, Connecticut: Keats Publishing Inc., 1972.

26. Jesen, Bernard, D.C., *Tissue Cleansing Through Bowel Management.* Escondido, California: Dr. Bernard Jensen, 1981.
27. Josephson, Elmer A., *God's Key to Health and Happiess.* Old Tappan, New Jersey: Fleming H. Revell Co., 1962.
28. Kirban, Salem, *How to Eat Your Way Back to Vibrant Health.* Huntingdon Valley, Pennsylvania: Salem Kirban Inc., 1977.
29. ____ *How to Keep Healthy and Happy by Fasting.* Huntingdon Valley, Pennsylvania: Salem Kirban Inc., 1976.
30. ____ *Health Guide for Survival.* Huntingdon Valley, Pennsylvania: Salem Kirban Inc., 1976.
31. Kirschner, H. E., M.D., *Live Food Juices.* Monrovia, California: H. E. Kirschner Publications, 1975.
32. ____ *Nature's Healing Grasses.* Riverside, California: H. C. White Publications.
33. ____ *Nature's Seven Doctors.* Riverside, California: H. C. White Publications, 1962.
34. Kulvinskas, Victoras, *Survival Into the 21st Century.* Wethersfield, Connecticut: Omangod Press, 1975.
35. ____ *Love Your Body.* Wethersfield, Connecticut: Omangod Press, 1974.
36. ____ *Life in the 21st Century.* Woodstock Valley, Connecticut: Omangod Press, 1981.
37. ____ *Sprout for the Love of Every Body.* Woodstock Valley, Connecticut: 1978.
38. Lovett, C. S., *Jesus Wants Us Well.* Baldwin Park, California: Personal Christianity, 1973.
39. Lust, John, *Drink Your Troubles Away.* New York: Benedict Lust Publications, 1967.
40. Mae, Edie, *How I Conquered Cancer Naturally.* Irvine, California: Harvest House Publications, 1975.
41. McDermott, Stella, *Metaphysics of Raw Foods.* Kansas City, Missouri: Burton Publishing Co., 1919.
42. Mendelsohn, Robert S., M.D., *Confessions of a Medical Heretic.* New York: Warner Books, 1980.
43. Nittler, Alan H., M.D., *A New Breed of Doctor.* New York: Pyramid House, 1972.
44. Parks, Mary June and Burgess, *Cooking for the Lord.* Frankfort, Kentucky: Park's Publishers, 1981.
45. Shelton, Herbert M., Ph.D., *Superior Nutrition.* San Antonio, Texas: Dr. Sheltons Health School, 1951.
46. ____ *Fasting Can Save Your Life.* Chicago: Natural Hygiene Society, 1964.
47. ____ *Food Combining Made East.* Chicago: Natural Hygiene Society, 1976.
48. Sherman, Ingrid, *Natural Remedies for Better Health.* Healdsburg, California: Naturegraph Publishers, 1970.
49. Swope, Mary Ruth, B.S., M.S., D.SC., *Green Leaves of Barley.* Melbourne, Florida: National Preventive Health Services, 1987.
50. ____ *Nutrition for Christians.* Melbourne, Florida: Swope Enterprises, Inc., 1981.

51. _____ *Are You Sick and Tired of Feeling Sick and Tired?* Pittsburg: Whitaker House, 1984.
52. Szekely, Edmond, *Treasury of Raw Foods.* Costa Rica, South America: International Biogenic Society, 1978.
53. Thomas, Luke Gordan, *Dying at 60 Youthful at 90.* Tracy, California: Plains Corporation, 1983.
54. Tilden, John H., M.D., *Toxemia The Basic Cause of Disease.* Chicago: Natural Hygiene Press, 1974.
55. Trop, Jack D., *Please Don't Smoke in Our House.* Chicago: Natural Hygiene Press, 1976.
56. United States Senate Report, *Dietary Goals for the United States.* Washington, D.C.: Government Printing Office, 1977.
57. Walker, N. W., D.SC., *Become Younger.* Phoenix, Arizona: Norwalk Press, 1949.
58. _____ *Diet and Salad Suggestions.* Phoenix, Arizona: Norwalk Press, 1971.
59. _____ *Vibrant Health.* Phoenix, Arizona: Norwalk Press, 1972.
60. _____ *Water Can Undermine Your Health.* Phoenix, Arizona: Norwalk Press, 1974.
61. _____ *Fresh Vegetables and Fruit Juices.* Phoenix, Arizona: Norwalk Press, 1978.
62. _____ *Colon Cancer.* Phoenix, Arizona: Norwalk Press, 1979.
63. _____ *Back to the Land.* Phoenix, Arizona: Norwalk Press, 1977.
64. _____ *Natural Weight Control.* Phoenix, Arizona: Norwalk Press, 1981.
65. West, C. Samuel, D.N., N.D., *The Golden Seven Plus One.* Orem, Utah: Samuel Publishing, 1981.
66. Wigmore, Ann, D.D., N.D., *Be Your Own Doctor.* Boston: Hippocrates Press, 1973.
67. _____ *Why Suffer.* Boston: Hippocrates PRess, 1984.
68. _____ *Hippocrates Live Food Program.* Boston: Hippocrates Press, 1984.
69. _____ *The Wheatgrass Book.* Wayne, New Jersey: Avery Publishing Group, Inc., 1985.
70. _____ *The Hippocrates Diet.* Wayne, New Jersey: Avery Publishing Group, Inc., 1984.